Class, Structure and Knowledge

Class, Structure and Knowledge

Problems in the Sociology of Knowledge

NICHOLAS ABERCROMBIE

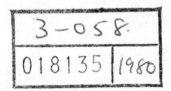
Basil Blackwell · Oxford

For my Father

Michael Abercrombie

First published 1980 by
Basil Blackwell Publisher
5 Alfred Street
Oxford OX1 4HB
England

British Library Cataloguing in Publication Data
Abercrombie, Nicholas
    Class, structure and knowledge.
    1. Knowledge, Sociology of
    I. Title
    301.2′1   BD175

    ISBN 0-631-12291-5
    ISBN 0-631-12301-5 Pbk

Typesetting by Malvern Typesetting Services
Printed in Great Britain by Billing and Sons Ltd
Guildford, London, Oxford, Worcester

Contents

Acknowledgements

For the preparation of this book I owe thanks to many people. Specifically I am indebted to Salvador Giner, Brian Longhurst, Bryan Turner, and John Urry, for making valiant efforts to save me from my own errors; to Bryan Wilson for many helpful, and detailed, suggestions; to my students, particularly the group graduating in 1978; to the Department of Sociology at Lancaster University for providing a stimulating environment in which to work; to Brenda Wright and Sylvia Stackhouse for typing the manuscript; to BA for being there; and to RA and JA for not coming in too often. None of these people are responsible for any errors which remain in my text.

Introduction

The sociology of knowledge is in an odd position as a specialized branch of sociology. It is potentially an important area of substantive analysis, being concerned to explain a wide variety of forms of belief from science to religion. At the same time it raises important *theoretical* questions for sociology generally, about the nature of sociological knowledge for example, which should put it at the centre of sociological theory. Yet, despite this centrality, the subject lacks both theoretical definition and substantive analysis. There are few textbooks or introductory books[1] and those that there are agree only on the most general principles. Theoretical debates on the subject tend not to go beyond simple programmatic statements about the relation of society and knowledge, or concentrate, almost obsessively, on the way in which sociological explanations of particular beliefs appear to cast doubt on the validity of the beliefs. Empirical analyses, on the other hand, tend to be isolated from one another and do not contribute to a continuing debate which might help in the construction of theory.

This relative neglect means that the subject has been relatively untouched by some of the recent trends in sociology, those involving quantitative methods or functionalism, for example. The subject is still effectively dominated by a very loosely organized set of principles largely derived from the work of one man, Karl Mannheim, whose main contributions were written in the 1920s and 1930s. This insulation of the sociology of knowledge from theoretical changes in sociology generally is a great pity. In particular, recent developments in the Marxist theory of ideology are plainly very relevant to the sociology of knowledge although fruitful intellectual contact is bedevilled by a mutual antipathy. It is true that the conventional position in the sociology of knowledge is heavily influenced by Marx, partly via the work of Mannheim. However this influence is actually dependent on a particular interpretation of Marx's writings, an interpretation largely rejected by contemporary Marxist theorists. Any debate between the conventional sociology of knowledge and the recent Marxist theory of ideology is therefore a debate between two conflicting readings of Marx.

Phenomenology, another recent tendency within sociological theory, has not entirely passed the sociology of knowledge by. Berger and Luckmann,[2] authors clearly within the phenomenological tradition, have attempted to rewrite the sociology of knowledge in a phenomenological way. However, again, the debate which they initiated has not been continued in such a way that one could form a view of the advantages that their reconstitution of the subject provides.

This book is an attempt to correct the isolation of the sociology of knowledge by contrasting it, on the one hand, with the Marxist theory of ideology, and, on the other, with phenomenology.

The Definition of the Sociology of Knowledge

As I have indicated, definitions of the subject tend to be both vague and general. Merton, for example, in a review of the sociology of knowledge, suggests that it is 'concerned with the relations between knowledge and other existential factors in the society or culture'.[3] Macquet argues that all work in the sociology of knowledge attempts to answer 'the three questions of the sociology of knowledge. What are the social or cultural factors which influence knowledge? What are the cognitive mental productions influenced? What is the degree and kind of conditioning between the two?'[4] Even more broadly, Berger and Luckmann claim that 'in so far as all human "knowledge" is developed, transmitted, and maintained in social situations, the sociology of knowledge must seek to understand the processes by which this is done in such a way that a taken-for-granted "reality" congeals for the man in the street. In other words, we contend that the *sociology of knowledge is concerned with the analysis of the social construction of* reality.'[5]

These definitions indicate not only that the subject lacks theoretical specificity, perhaps not surprising in sociology, but also that it makes ambitious claims. Thus 'knowledge' is interpreted widely; all sorts of beliefs are thought susceptible of sociological analysis. Included in the subject are studies of moral and empirical claims, true and false beliefs, scientific theories, and literary works. As will be seen, this generality of aim creates problems of various kinds. Symptomatic of these are the confusions surrounding the term 'ideology'. In the view of some authors, this concept refers to a particular *kind* of belief. Shils, for example, says: 'Ideologies are characterized by a high degree of explicitness of formulation over a very wide range of the subjects with which they deal. . . . As compared with other patterns of belief, ideologies are relatively highly systematized or integrated around one or a few preeminent values, such as salvation, equality, or ethnic purity.'[6] In addition, they emphasize their distinctiveness, they demand individual subservience and a corporate collective form of organization of adherents. These features distinguish ideologies from other systems of belief such as creeds, outlooks or programmes which all tend to be less explicit, less organized around a central belief, less closed to innovation, less invested with emotion, and not so tightly associated with a corporate body of devotees. Perhaps the most important characteristic of ideologies is that they 'passionately oppose the productions of the cultural institutions of the central institutional system'.[7] An ideology exists partly through its opposition to central values, either seeking a total transformation of those values or a total withdrawal from them. This oppositional character invests all ideologies with a necessarily political quality; however remote their direct concerns may seem to be from government, the fact that they have to strike an attitude towards the central value system politicizes them.

This narrow conception of ideology as a highly systematized and oppositional body of beliefs tends to go together with a functionalist type of explanation. Thus Shils holds that ideology is a response to a particular need of the personality, the need for intellectual order. Apter suggests that ideology has two functions, 'one directly social, binding the community together, and the other individual, organizing the role personalities of the maturing individual'.[8] However different are the rival explanations, they all have in common the same explanatory target, namely a very particular *kind* of belief, which they call ideology. Such a conception of ideology entails a comparison, often only implicit, with non-ideological thought, a comparison which tends to be drawn partly in evaluative terms. Thus, for Shils, ideologies are epitomized by Nazism and Bolshevism, while for Parsons, they are marked by a disregard for fundamental scientific procedures.[9] In other words ideologies, being closed-minded, irrational and unscientific, are contrasted with thought that is calm, measured and scientific. Politically the contrast is between doctrines that emphasize authoritarianism, dogmatism and violence, and those that stress democracy and freedom. There are, of course, a number of difficulties in drawing contrasts of this kind. A more important drawback to the narrow conception of ideology, however, is the way in which it diverts sociological attention away from non-ideological thought. Ideologies, being exotic growths, are seen 'naturally' to attract enquiry.

There are other approaches that interpret the word 'ideology', much more widely, as any system of belief produced under particular social circumstances, or, indeed, simply any system of belief. Plamenatz, for example, thinks that the contemporary sense of ideology 'is used to refer to a set of closely related beliefs or ideas, or even attitudes, characteristic of a group or community' (the sense of the term being used in this book).[10] Ideologies therefore have a systemic quality; they 'hang together' in some way. Conceived in this way, 'we can enquire into the spread of an ideology, what sort of people or what proportion of a people or of mankind share it, or we can enquire into its comprehensiveness, into the proportion of their total ideas and attitudes that it covers. An ideology may be widely spread and be either very comprehensive or not so'.[11] Many Marxists, though not all, while agreeing that ideology must be conceived in a fairly general way, would argue that the term should be restricted to those systems of belief that are in some sense false or distorted, qualities that are produced by certain social situations. Such a view necessarily involves a distinction between ideological thought and science, the latter giving the vantage point from which ideology can be identified and studied.

The same word, 'ideology', is thus interpreted in both a narrow and a wide way, interpretations which produce very different theories of knowledge. The simultaneous employment of both causes considerable confusion, aptly illustrated in the so-called 'End of Ideology' debate. In the 1950s, a number of authors[12] argued, first, that the nature of Western industrial societies had changed radically over the previous one hundred years, and secondly, that the character of public political debate had also changed. Lipset, for example, suggested that the system of representative democracy has permitted the solution of the social problems generated by the industrial revolution. There may still be political tensions, but these do not relate to fundamental divisions in society; those have gone for ever. As a consequence, political debate is not nearly so sharp; it tends to be over such questions as the price of milk rather than over the nature of the good society. In other words, political argument is no longer ideological; we have reached the end of ideology. As Bell says, 'Few serious minds believe any longer that one can set down "blueprints" and through "social engineering" bring about a new Utopia of social harmony.'[13] Plainly, Bell has a narrow conception of ideology in mind here; at the forefront of his argument is the decline of Marxist and socialist beliefs. There is a great deal wrong with this argument but unfortunately quite a few of the opponents of the End of Ideology Thesis understood ideology in a much wider sense and took the thesis to be claiming that ideologies of all kinds were disappearing, a much more implausible claim.

The Sociology of Knowledge and the History of Ideas

As an academic discipline, the sociology of knowledge seems readily comparable to the history of ideas. Both subjects are interested in accurate descriptions of systems of ideas and, much more significantly, in demonstrating similarities between doctrines that at first sight will be dissimilar. According to Lovejoy,[14] the history of ideas can be constructed around the concept of the unit-idea. Such ideas are elemental, the basic building blocks out of which whole systems of ideas may be constructed. The identification of these units makes possible comparison of doctrines remote from one another in space and time. In his book *The Great*

Chain of Being,[15] for example, Lovejoy argues that over a very long period, from Plato to the late eighteenth century, most educated men held a view of the structure of the world which informed all their thinking, whether it was religious, scientific, philosophical, artistic, or literary. This view was that all the things in the world are arranged in a hierarchy, or Chain of Being, from God at the top to the lowest kind of creature. There were an infinite number of links in the chain, which was itself, at the same time, infinitely long. An important conclusion then is that the history of ideas like the sociology of knowledge is, to some extent, an exercise in 'unmasking', looking behind the very diverse things people say to the common elements of which the people themselves may be unaware.

This important methodological similarity should not, however, obscure the differences in the practices of the two disciplines. The first difference is that historians of ideas turn out to be more interested in *description*; in detecting unit-ideas and showing how particular notions persist through time. There is relatively little interest in *explanation*, in showing, for example, why it is that people should hold one set of ideas rather than another, or in explaining why some unit-ideas persist while others do not. Further, when explanation is provided, it often tends to be of a markedly unsociological kind. Thus changes in ideas are attributed not to underlying social factors but to the process of intellectual discovery and debate. Explanation in the history of ideas tends to be in terms of the ideas themselves; the sources of change are located 'internally' to the systems of ideas not 'externally' in non-intellectual factors.[16] A remark of Lovejoy will serve to illustrate this tendency: 'Now if Plato had stopped here, the subsequent history of Western thought would, it can hardly be doubted, have been profoundly different from what it has been.'[17] One can hardly imagine a sociologist agreeing with this estimate of the independent causal importance of Plato's doctrine in itself, over a long period of time, and in societies of greatly different social and economic complexions. However there might well be some agreement that certain basic and very general notions will underlie systems of thought and may give form to more specific propositions. Indeed, it is part of the sociologist's task to identify these basic ideas as the preliminary to their explanation.

The Development of the Subject

In a very general way then, the sociology of knowledge involves looking behind expressed beliefs to some social base. However, such a move is not restricted to the academic discipline. In the debates of everyday life, opponents may often not refer to the content of the arguments themselves but instead to a set of interests or dispositions which are thought to structure or produce the arguments. Usually this position will refer to individual or psychological states. Thus it is not uncommon to hear people say of some argument such things as 'that is a self-interested remark'. Again it may also be thought that it is membership of a social group that is responsible for what a person says as in the claim 'that is a characteristically male argument'.

Given the way that arguments of this kind are used in everyday life, it is perhaps not surprising that theories of the social determination of knowledge appeared long before the comparatively recent institutionalization of sociology as an academic discipline. For example, Bacon believed that men's perceptions of the world were shaped by various kinds of preconceptions or 'idols'.[18] Firstly, there are idols of the tribe by which the 'light of nature' is distorted by the fact of belonging to the human species; 'man's sense is falsely asserted to be the standard of things'.[19] Secondly, the 'idols of the den derive their origin from the peculiar nature of each individual's mind and body, and also from education, habit and accident'.[20] Thirdly, there are 'idols formed by the reciprocal intercourse and society of man with man, which we call idols of the market, from the commerce and association of men with each other'.[21] Lastly, there are the idols of the theatre 'that have crept into men's minds from the various dogmas of peculiar systems of philosophy and also from the perverted rules of demonstration'.[22] Bacon's notion is, then, that our understanding of the objective, given, external world is obstructed by socially created qualities of the mind which act as mental filters. His solution is the reformation of scientific technique, so as to minimize the role of the individual intelligence, while maximizing that of impersonal instruments and equipment.

Much later, most of the writers of the classical period of sociology made contributions to the sociology of knowledge, although this was often incidental to the production of more general sociological theories rather than the creation of a specific theory of knowledge. For example in Pareto's distinction between residues and deviations, there is an implicit, if crude, sociology of knowledge. Pareto divides human action into two domains, the logical and the non-logical. Science, a fairly limited area, is characterized by careful observation, logical argument, and controlled experimentation; non-logical action is that action not informed by these principles. It is the second area that commands Pareto's interest, for it is the most significant socially since the social importance of action is not determined by the truth or logic of the beliefs which sustain it. To explain non-logical action Pareto appeals to a set of 'sentiments' which are constants of human nature rather like instincts. Sentiments are not manifested directly in social behaviour but appear as 'residues', 'just as the rising of the mercury in a thermometer is a manifestation of the rise in temperature'. So a set of constants, residues, which Pareto lists in great detail, produce the great range and diversity of non-logical action. However, more important for our present purposes is that man has an intrinsic need to make his non-logical actions appear logical and to this end he develops all sorts of justifications, explanations and theories. These Pareto calls 'derivations' which are, like non-logical actions, ultimately traceable to the residues or sentiments. Thus, in the theory of residues and derivations, there is an attempt to explain beliefs (derivations) in terms of some non-intellectual, quasi-social factors (residues).

Central to Durkheim's project is an opposition to any form of sociological analysis which takes the individual as its starting point. Society is not a simple aggregate of individuals but is a separate reality in its own right. Instead of considering the way in which society is constructed out of the actions of individual persons, we should look at the manner in which individuals are formed by society even in respect of 'the style of our houses'. Such a programme has to solve the problem of explaining the social origin of beliefs, ideas and theories which, at first sight, seem quintessentially individual. Durkheim does this primarily by investigation of religious belief, trying to relate the form of religious experience and worship to the form of the society in which they are located. However, much more ambitiously, he also attempts to show how the most central categories of thought like space, time and number, are socially determined. Time, for example, 'expresses the rhythm of the collective activities' in that 'The divisions into days, weeks, months, years etc. correspond to the periodical recurrence of rites, feasts, and public ceremonies.'[23] Similarly space is a socially derived category: 'There are societies in Australia and North America where space is conceived in the form of an immense circle, because the camp has a circular form.'[24] Concepts such as space and time are therefore neither *a priori* nor are they constructed out of sense experience by the *individual* intellect. They are instead 'the result of an immense cooperation . . . to make them a multitude of minds have associated, united and combined their ideas and sentiments . . . A special intellectual activity is therefore concentrated in them which is infinitely richer and complexer than that of the individual'.[25]

For Pareto and Durkheim, then, as indeed for Marx and Weber, a sociology of knowledge was simply part of the more general sociological enterprise.

The elevation of the subject into a specialized branch of sociology is due primarily to the later work of Mannheim. As it has developed, the sociology of knowledge has become dominated by one approach deriving from Mannheim, who in turn drew heavily on a particular interpretation of Marx. This, by now conventional position, which I shall call the Marx–Mannheim position, has informed practically all theoretical and substantive work in the sociology of knowledge until comparatively recently. The next two chapters will be devoted to expounding the conventional argument. Its basic tenets are as follows. The kinds of beliefs that people hold are determined (though perhaps not solely determined) by the social groups of which they are members; the social group in effect provides an environment in which the beliefs are learnt. Social groups are not of equal causal importance in the determination of beliefs and, in any case, it is plain that people are members of various, cross-cutting groups. In feudal and capitalist societies, the most significant group is class and one might generally expect beliefs to vary with class membership. However, the problem is not merely to show that certain beliefs are associated with certain social classes, it is also to explain why one *particular* set of beliefs, rather than any other, goes together with a *particular* social class.

Generally, the Marx–Mannheim position utilizes the concept of interest as the explanatory mechanism; social classes adopt sets of beliefs as those beliefs further the interests of that class.

An account of this conventional position in the sociology of knowledge is the starting point of this book, which is structured as a debate between the conventional position and two groups of critics who are discussed in Parts II and III. On the one hand, recent Marxist writers object to the narrowness of the conception of belief employed by the orthodox theory and they further hold that the concepts of class and class-interest are too superficial as explanatory concepts. On the other hand, writers inspired by the phenomenological approach object both to the neglect of common-sense knowledge and belief and also to the conception of social structure as a force which constrains and determines the human subject. The book is not intended, therefore, as a history of the sociology of knowledge, nor as an overview of all the debates within the subject, but is rather an analysis of some of the problems raised in one, if the most dominant, perspective.

I
The Conventional Position

There are several sociologies of knowledge that can be extracted from Marx's work. In this book I shall be interested in two of them. The first, which will be presented in this section, is that which has been conventionally presented until recently as *the* sociology of knowledge. The second, which is a critique deriving from many different sources, is discussed in Part II.

Marx did not write a book on the sociology of knowledge. The result is that we have to look in different parts of his work in order to construct such a sociology. This is not a deficiency in Marx since he would not have recognized the need for a separate theory of ideology at all; such a theory is simply entailed by a number of his other views. For example, one of the things that interests Marx most in his earlier works[1] is the construction of a general theory of history, a materialist view, in which the moving force consists of the forces and relations of production; if we wish to explain historical change, then ultimately we must look at changes in the means of production and changes in the relations between men as they are involved in the means of production. To some extent this view is presented polemically since Marx wants to refute an alternative account of history, one in which its moving force is the consciousness of men, their ideas, intentions, motives and principles. Thus the Young Hegelians 'consider conceptions, thoughts, ideas, in fact all the products of consciousness, to which they attribute an independent existence, as the real chains of men . . .'.[2] Again, Proudhon is criticized for seeing history as the unfolding of great principles such as authority or individualism.

Marx's critique of these idealist accounts of history involves the provision of a theory *explaining* the origin of the ideas that the Young Hegelians, for example, believed to be the motors of history:

> In direct contrast to german philosophy which descends from heaven to earth, here we ascend from earth to heaven. That is to say, we do not set out from what men say, imagine, conceive, nor from men as narrated, thought of, imagined, conceived, in order to arrive at men in the flesh. We set out from real, active men, and on the basis of their real life-process we demonstrate the development of the ideological reflexes and echoes of this life process.[3]

Crudely, ideas do not cause changes in the material conditions of men, the material conditions of men cause changes in ideas. So the materialist view of history contains the outline of a theory of ideology. I have referred to a conventional account of Marx's views on the social determination of knowledge. More precisely, this account actually contains two separate doctrines, each with a distinctive starting point in Marx's writings. The first of these is encapsulated in the phrase 'social being determines consciousness' and the second in 'base determines superstructure'. Although most Marxist theories of knowledge and culture would like to see themselves as reconciling these two doctrines, actually there is a systematic tension between them which can prove awkward.

Class-Interest and Ideology

The orthodox starting place for a Marxist sociology of knowledge is the formula from the Preface to *A Contribution to the Critique of Political Economy*: 'It is not the consciousness of men that determines their being, but, on the contrary, their social being that determines their consciousness.'[4] As I suggested at the beginning of this chapter, this kind of remark by Marx is intended polemically and requires some interpretation. At the least, Marx plainly means to say that consciousness is not some free-floating autonomous element but can be partially explained by reference to 'social being'. But what is meant by 'social being'? Although in the Preface this phrase seems to refer to some rather unspecified category such as the 'social conditions of man's existence', what is in fact crucial to the determination of beliefs is an element of social being, namely 'the mode of production of material life'. So it is man's involvement in a particular mode of production of goods and services that determines his beliefs. However this formulation is still not adequate for we do not know what constitutes 'involvement'. Men are involved in a mode of production to the extent that the mode is embedded in a set of social relations—in the relations of production—and, in particular, in the system of social class relationships. A particular social class is involved in particular ways in a mode of production; social class determines consciousness. For any one individual it is his membership in a social class, *as that class has a certain position in a mode of production that determines* his beliefs. As Marx puts it in *The Eighteenth Brumaire of Louis Bonaparte*:

> Upon the different forms of property, upon the social conditions of existence, rises an entire superstructure of distinct and peculiarly formed sentiments, illusions, modes of thought and views of life. The entire class creates and forms them out of its material foundations and out of the corresponding social relations. The single individual, derives them through tradition and upbringing.[5]

A reading of the original formula as 'social class, as it is involved in a mode of production, determines consciousness' requires further elucidation in that the meaning of both 'determines' and 'consciousness' is unclear. To say that A determines B is plainly to say that there is some kind of causal relationship between A and B. Commentators on Marx have assumed that the character of B is entirely and exclusively fixed by A,[6] that given someone's class one can more or less read off their beliefs. One familiar way of understanding 'determine' is in terms of causal importance; to say that A determines B is to say that in the formation of B, A is causally important, more important than any other element, but not the only element contributing to B. In the formation of beliefs, classes are of crucial, but not final, causal importance. However not all kinds of belief are equally causally influenced by class. Marx occasionally speaks as though natural science and logic are categories of consciousness removed from determination by class or the mode of production. Engels is even more specific in suggesting that those beliefs most involved in the productive process will be most influenced by class; aesthetic doctrines, for example, will be less shaped by class and more by other factors than will economic theories. So far I have read the basic formula of 'social being determines consciousness' as meaning 'social class, as it is involved in a mode of production, is of great causal importance in the formation of beliefs, more so for some kinds of belief than for others'. The other factors that may be involved in the formation of beliefs are not therefore necessarily reducible to class.

In one respect the analysis so far is rather artificial. In representing the theory as a causal theory, I have more or less suggested that what a conventional Marxist sociology of knowledge seeks to do is to describe the causal influences in the formation of any individual's belief-system and it seeks to locate the answer primarily in terms of social class *membership*. It can be argued, however, that such an approach is at altogether too superficial a level and that what is required is an analysis of the constitution of, and relations between, modes of production in a society, which will show how both social classes and systems of belief are effects of these relations. This point will be taken up again in Part II.

To say that 'social class, as it is involved in a mode of production, is of great causal importance in the formation of beliefs' is still not theoretically adequate, for it does not tell us what causal mechanism is involved. What precisely is the link between membership in a social class and belief, or between a social class and the belief-system 'appropriate' to it? The answer lies in a particular use of the notion of *interest*, a notion crucial to conventional Marxist theories of belief, though unfortunately more often assumed than explicated.

Marx himself used interest in all sorts of different ways. He discussed the conflicts of interest between individuals and individuals, between individuals and the State, between individuals and the social classes of which they are members, between different elements within a social class, between different aspirations of a class, and between social class and social class. Despite this variety of use, however, in the *abstract* analysis of the sociology of knowledge it is the way that social classes conflict that is of importance: 'How is it that personal interests always develop, against the will of individuals into class-interests, into common interests which acquire independent existence in relation to the individual persons, and in their independence assume the form of general interests?'[7] However for the solution of a particular problem in a 'specific society at a specific time', Marx speaks of the interests of many different kinds of *groups*. In the *Eighteenth Brumaire*, for example, one of the most important features in the analysis is the way that different sections of the bourgeoisie, the landowners and the finance capitalists, have apparently quite different systems of belief, but, despite these differences, the basic difference underlying all the others, and the one which is ultimately the most important socially, is the conflict of interest and belief between the bourgeoisie, as a whole, and the proletariat.

Marx's discussion of interest implies a distinction between 'subjective interests', which are simply those wants, aspirations and preferences that people actually express, and 'real interests',[8] which people may be said to have even if they are unaware of them and which they may actually deny. In opposition to the Marxist position, which takes real interests seriously, many political theorists believe that it is analytically absurd, and even morally disagreeable, to speak of real interests as something separate from expressed wants; it has the absurdity that is often felt in everyday life when someone says that he knows what is in someone else's 'best interests'. The traditional argument against real interests is that their ascription to any class or group is arbitrary; we have no reason for ascribing any one interest to a group rather than another; any such ascription merely depends on the personal preferences of the person making the ascription. The only way we have of deciding what a person's or group's interests are is to look at what they *say* their interests (or wants) are. Thus the only meaningful notion of interests is the subjective one.

It might be possible to construct a sociology of belief based on subjective interest as the causal mechanism but it would, I think, be rather uninteresting. It would, for example, make it difficult to say that beliefs were at variance with interests. However there are other serious difficulties in treating subjective interest as the only conception of interest. Firstly, it must be possible to be mistaken as to one's interest. Thus a man can have a want and favour a policy which he believes will satisfy that want, but be mistaken about the actual effectiveness of that policy. In this case, although he might declare that the policy is in his interests, in fact he is wrong. Secondly, it does seem possible, superficially at least, to have interests of which one is not aware. Thus some sense ought to attach to saying that it is not in a man's interests to drink six bottles of whisky a day (particularly if he does not know the effect). Typically, in everyday life, such arguments are used about children who may do things 'not in their interests', the assumption being that they do not know what they are doing. Thirdly, an empirical difficulty is that it may actually be difficult for people to express their wants; they may simply be unable to articulate them.

These are reasons for wanting to go beyond the notion of interest as merely subjective; for wanting to say that interest is not merely equivalent to expressed wants. However there is a more powerful argument. The suggestion that interest is equivalent to expressed wants assumes that wants are 'given'. A sociologist, however, is going to want to see wants not as random but as caused; he will look for the social structural elements that 'give' people one set of wants rather than another. In an extreme case, this claim would be designed to take account of a society in which people were manipulated (by some form of mass-hypnosis, perhaps) into wanting, for example, an endless stream of consumer durables such that they replace their car every week. In such an event, one would be inclined to say that people were being forced into having 'false' wants. However, duress of this kind is only an extreme possibility, for in *any* society it is the case that people acquire their wants from somewhere; they are always *learnt* not given. One cannot therefore take expressed wants as given but must enquire into their sources.

These points indicate that any concept of real interests has firstly to be tied to wants in *some* way; there have to be *some* circumstances in which people will want what is said to be in their interests.[9] Secondly the concept is an essentially comparative one in that we have to have a definition which states a situation in which it is possible for people to *choose* between sets of wants. The account of real interest provided by Connolly goes some way towards a satisfactory definition. 'Policy x is more in A's interest than policy y if A, were he to experience the results of both x and y, would choose x as the result he would rather have for himself.'[10] This definition does make the choices of the agent the ultimate arbiter of interest but does recognize that wants are socially produced. However it is not arbitrary since it is possible to conceive of a test which would falsify any one ascription of interest. It is true, certainly, that such a test would be difficult to carry out, requiring as it does that 'investigators . . . make different judgements, in many situations, about the choices a person would make if he had had the relevant experience'.[11]

So the suggestion is that interest, particularly class-interest, shapes belief or, more specifically, that beliefs are adopted which *further* class-interest. One further characteristic of the *logic* of the connection between interests and beliefs should be noted. This is that the relationship between interest and belief is essentially functionalist; the claim is that beliefs *function* to support, in some way, the interest of the class espousing the beliefs. This raises the problem of whether interest-explanations are really causal, although it is plain that conventional Marxist theories believe that they are. This point is discussed at the end of this chapter.

To the extent that interest forms belief, the belief is 'distorted'. The distortion takes two forms. Firstly, the beliefs will morally represent only one 'narrow' interest; moral claims will be made which in fact favour only one sector of the population even if they pretend to be more generally beneficial. Free competition for example, may be advanced as a virtue applicable to everybody, when it provides greater benefits for entrepreneurs than for workers. But there will also be empirical distortion. Class-interest narrows the vision and men may see only part of the world. Systems of belief may be regularly confirmed as true, but still provide only a partial account of reality. In fact, of course, it is practically impossible to talk of belief-systems in the real world as straightforwardly *empirically* false, since they are composed of moral claims as well as factual statements. The best that one can do is to represent them as potentially *partial* in that both moral and empirical claims support each other in furthering the relevant interest. As Marx says: '. . . liberal phrases are the idealistic expression of the real interests of the bourgeoisie . . .',[12] where liberal phrases are both empirical and moral claims. Marx also draws attention to one particular feature of interest-related beliefs, namely that they attempt to disguise their own nature. Thus classes attempt to present policies or beliefs which are in fact in their own special interests as being in the general interest.

Many Marxists, when they talk of the way that interests distort systems of beliefs, speak simultaneously of 'false consciousness'. The supposition is, that to the extent that men's interests shape their beliefs, they are falsely conscious. All men are falsely conscious, at least in societies which have modes of production that generate social classes with specific interests; if there were social classes without interests, they would not be falsely conscious. We are thus given a criterion of false consciousness dependent on some notion of distortion, although, as we have seen, it is by no means a straightforward one.

Unfortunately, the literature on the sociology of knowledge treats the concept of false consciousness in a definitely ambiguous way,[13] in that it defines the concept both in terms of distortion *and* in terms of pursuit of interest. For this latter criterion, a set of beliefs represents a false consciousness to the extent that it does not further the interests of the class concerned. For example, if the working class in capitalist society tends to adopt the beliefs also adopted by the bourgeoisie, then it is falsely conscious. The use of both criteria gives paradoxical results. If a class adopts beliefs that do further its interests, it is simultaneously truly and falsely conscious. Clearly some terminological clarification is called for, and one possibility is to use false consciousness in the sense of falsity to the pursuit of interests. This proposal, however, would not rule out the use of the notion of the distortion of beliefs; quite the contrary, both notions have to be incorporated in the Marxist scheme. By putting both together, one can construct the following set of boxes.

	falsely conscious	truly conscious
'distortion' (appearance)	The proletariat in capitalist society	The bourgeoisie in capitalist society
'non-distortion' (reality)	Bourgeois socialists in a revolutionary situation	The proletariat in a revolutionary situation

This scheme itself generates some apparent paradoxes, particularly in labelling the bourgeoisie in capitalist society as truly conscious. It does however show the centrality of the concept of interest in a Marxist sociology of knowledge.

However, the classification reveals two further problems. Firstly, although the proletariat does have a 'distorted' system of beliefs and this distortion does indeed have something to do with interest, the mechanism involved turns out to be rather different from that which distorts the beliefs of the bourgeoisie. This problem is that traditionally raised in discussions of the 'base' and 'superstructure'. Secondly, I have not yet provided any account of how it is that 'non-distorted' beliefs are generated. This is the problem of how a Marxist 'science' can be provided.

Base and Superstructure

In the previous section, I started from the conventional formula, 'It is not the consciousness of men that determines their being but, on the contrary, their social being that determines their consciousness.' It would have been equally conventional to have had another starting point, namely, 'base determines superstructure'. Although they may give rather different results, these two starting points are certainly not radically different, for they effectively deal with the problem at different levels. The first gives us a way of looking at the belief-systems of social classes, while the second supplies an account of those beliefs that dominate a society.

We may start from Marx's Preface to *A Contribution to the Critique of Political Economy*:

> In the social production of their life, men enter into definite relations that are indispensable and independent of their will, relations of production which correspond to a definite stage of development of their material productive forces. The sum total of these relations of production constitutes the economic structure of society, the real foundation, on which rises a legal and political superstructure and to which correspond definite forms of social consciousness. [14]

There is therefore an economic base and a legal, political and ideational superstructure. The base is conventionally understood by commentators on Marx to comprise the forces plus the relations of production. For example, the former are siad by Mills to comprise:

> (a) natural resources, such as land and minerals, so far as they are used as objects of labour; (b) physical equipment such as tools, machines, technology; (c) science and engineering, the skills of men who invent and improve this equipment; (d) those who do work with these skills and tools; (e) their division of labour in so far as this social organisation increases their productivity. [15]

The relations of production are often seen as something over and above the forces of production, which is misleading, since Marx clearly says that different elements within the forces of production were related to each other in different ways, and it was *these relations* that constituted the relations of production. In any event, conventional accounts tend to interpret the relations of production in a rather more straightforward way, simply as *class* relations. Thus, according to Cole:

> Marx held that these relations between men and men, involving the definition of rights of property and personal freeaom and obligation, have in the past been embodied in successive class systems, so that each class system has corresponded to a particular stage in the development of the social use of the powers of production, including both things and men. [16]

The superstructure is then an avowedly residual category including political, educational and religious institutions, as well as all systems of belief.

So far I have left the exact relation between base and superstructure undefined. It is often suggested that Marx claimed that the base determines the superstructure, in that the dominant mode of production unequivocally determines the character of the beliefs current in the society. It is clear, however, that neither Marx nor Engels ever held such a doctrine. Firstly, they suggested that superstructural elements could be relatively autonomous of the base and have their own laws of development. Engels, for example, says that not all kinds of belief are equally determined by the base: 'The further the particular sphere we are investigating is removed from the economic sphere and approaches that of pure abstract ideology, the more shall we find it exhibiting accidents . . . in its development, the more will its course run in a zig-zag.'[17] Thus the forms taken by art and literature may be much less closely related to the economic base than will political or economic theories. Secondly, and more radically, Marx and Engels argue that the superstructure will interact with, or influence, the base. In *Capital*, for example, Marx is at pains to show the independent importance of beliefs about the conditions of work. There is no reason inherent in the nature of capital why the working day should be limited: '. . . apart from extremely elastic bounds, the nature of the exchange of commodities itself imposes no limit to the working day, no limit to surplus-labour'.[18] Nonetheless the length of the working day is regulated by the State, partially as the outcome of a struggle between competing classes and sets of beliefs. Again, as Engels points out:

> The economic situation is the basis, but the various elements of the superstructure—political forms of the class struggle and its results, to wit: constitutions established by the victorious class after a successful battle, etc, forms, and even the reflexes of all these actual struggles in the brains of the participants, political, juristic, philosophical theories, religious views . . . also exercise their influence upon the course of the historical struggles and in many cases preponderate in determining their *form*. There is an interaction of all these elements in which, amid all the endless hosts of accidents. . . . The economic movement finally asserts itself as necessary.[19]

Engels's conclusion is thus that the economic is of final and decisive importance but the superstructure may still influence the economic. Such a formulation does not give any precise guide as to the *relative* importance of the base and superstructure. This question will be taken up again in Part II.

It has often proved very difficult to maintain the conceptual distinctions which are involved in the conventional base and superstructure doctrine. Most of the difficulties centre on the notion of relations of production. Plamenatz,[20] for example, argues that conventional definitions of the relations of production do not make them independent of the superstructure which they are supposed to determine. Thus, in the quotation from Cole cited above, relations of production seem to involve the rights of property. Yet these rights, being legal conceptions, are also superstructual. Mills's account of the forces of production presents similar problems since it seems to make scientific theory and the social organization of labour constitutive of the forces of production, when there are good grounds for supposing them to be superstructual. This is a complex and somewhat technical problem and Marxist replies to Plamenatz's objection depend on very detailed discussion of the relations of production. Cohen's solution, for example, displays 'ownership' as a matter of enjoying rights and then tries to formulate a concept of a power that corresponds to each right. From these moves he believes that he can formulate a non-legal interpretation of the legal terms in Marx's characterization of production relations, in such a way that property relations can be explained by production relations.[21]

From the point of view of the sociology of knowledge, Marx's distinction in the Preface between base and superstructure is interpreted generally as saying that the *dominant* ideas of an epoch or society reflect (in some way to be defined) the *dominant* form of economic organization or more precisely, the dominant mode of production. For example, the various doctrines collectively referred to as individualism are often said to reflect the domination of the capitalist mode of production. Such doctrines emphasize the claims of the individual *vis-à-vis* some other entity such as the Church or the State and make him the final arbiter of his moral and political choices. Individualistic theories appeared in a number of different fields at different times. Thus religious individualism, effectively denying the importance of the Church as an intermediary between man and his God, appears significantly from about the fifteenth century onwards. The seventeenth and eighteenth centuries were the heyday of individualistic theories of political obligation, while individualism is a characteristic of the literature and economic theory of the eighteenth and early nineteenth centuries. It is suggested that individualism, as this very general *style* of thought, reflected capitalism in that that economic system has to treat people as autonomous economic units formally equal and separate as buyers and sellers in a market.

I suggested earlier that the relations of production are often interpreted simply as *class* relations. This has turned the notion that the dominant ideas of a society somehow reflect the dominant mode of production into the argument that the dominant ideas are the ideas of the dominant *class*. The inspiration for this position comes from *The German Ideology*:

> The ideas of the ruling class are in every epoch the ruling ideas: i.e. the class which is the ruling material force of society, is at the same time its ruling intellectual force. The class which has the means of material production at its disposal, has control at the same time over the means of mental production, so that thereby, generally speaking, the ideas of those who lack the means of mental production are subject to it. The ruling ideas are nothing more than the ideal expression of the dominant material relationships grasped as ideas . . . Insofar, therefore, as they (the individuals of the ruling class) rule as a class and determine the extent and compass of an epoch, it is self-evident that they do this in its whole range, hence among other things rule also as thinkers, as producers of ideas, and regulate the production and distribution of the ideas of their age. Thus their ideas are the ruling ideas of an epoch. For instance, in an age and in a country where royal power, aristocracy and bourgeoisie are contending for mastery, the doctrine of the separation of powers proves to be the dominant idea and is expressed in an eternal law.[22]

This 'ruling ideas' doctrine has been interpreted in two ways. There is firstly a weak interpretation which suggests that the dominant class settle only what ideas are to be prominent or obvious in a society. There may well be other beliefs or opinions current that may in fact be held by the majority, but they will not come to public view because the ruling class has command over the means of the production and distribution of ideas. This interpretation of the ruling ideas doctrine is common in Marxist studies of culture and is implicit in Marx's stricture concerning any attempt at a complete interpretation of an age merely by examination of the ideas publicly prevalent at the time; he suggests that the subterranean ideas of a subordinate class are equally worthy of examination. In studies of this kind, the role of intellectuals as producers and disseminators of ruling ideas is critical, and it is theoretically possible for the intellectual stratum to come adrift from the ruling class. In such circumstances the dominant ideas (in the sense of the obvious ideas) may not be those of the ruling class. One must therefore qualify the ruling ideas doctrine by suggesting that the dominant class and the apparatus of the distribution of ideas must be conceptualized separately. I shall be considering the importance of this separation in later chapters.[23]

Sociologists interested in politics may adopt a rather stronger interpretation of the passage from *The German Ideology*. It may be the case that the dominant class is able to ensure that their ideas are the only ones that are publicly available, but it may also be true that they are able to *impose* those ideas on other classes in such a way that all members of a society think in ruling class categories. For example, in contemporary societies it may be that the educational system is so imbued with dominant ideas that subordinate classes are literally unable to *formulate* their opposition; the prevalence of dominant ideas impedes dissent. Thus it is suggested that the working class in Britain are politically conformist because of their adoption of such dominant ideas as the importance of nation over class or the sanctity of private property.

This model of the impact of the dominant ideas of a society on the subordinate classes is very common in conventional Marxist theories of knowledge. However, apart from the very important methodological difficulty of identifying in a concrete instance what body of beliefs forms the dominant ideology, there are two assumptions which require further examination. These are: (1) that the dominated classes do hold dominant beliefs and (2) that it is irrelevant whether or not the ruling class hold the dominant beliefs.[24] There is little evidence for the first of these assumptions. In the feudal period, for example, in which religion is said to be the dominant ideology, the peasantry were not noted for their religious devotion, and religious conceptions such as the 'Great Chain of Being' that might have had political uses were better known to the ruling classes. In fact the mechanisms of ideological incorporation were not especially efficient since the Church had to cope both with a lack of literacy and with differences in spoken language. Similar points can be made for the earlier phases of capitalism in which likely candidates for elements of dominant ideology like individualism or 'Victorian morality' were not characteristic beliefs of the working classes. Even Methodism, so often thought of as the opiate of the masses, was a relatively small and petit-bourgeois movement. It is only with the later phases of capitalism, with the development of a system of mass education, that the techniques of transmission of the dominant ideology become at all efficient. Even in contemporary society, however, it would be incorrect to assume that the working classes have a false consciousness induced by their acceptance of a dominant ideology. The best conception of working class belief-systems is that they represent a 'dual consciousness' in which dominant conceptions sit uneasily alongside dissenting ones.[25]

Indeed, in feudalism and early capitalism it would be more correct to say that it was the dominant class that 'really' believed the dominant ideology and that the available apparatus of ideological transmission seemed almost aimed at them; both the Church and the limited educational system have the effect of ensuring a much higher degree of ideological coherence in the dominant class than was remotely possible in the subordinate classes. These empirical points may indicate the necessity of some theoretical alteration in the ruling ideas model. It may well be that the dominant ideology functions chiefly towards the *dominant* class, perhaps in securing the measure of social coherence necessary for the preservation, transmission, and accumulation of private property so important in the feudal and early capitalist period.[26] This would not, however, be to deny that the relative availability of dominant ideas might have the *secondary* effect of partially incorporating the subordinate classes. However, even with the last qualification, these arguments suggest that any simple conception of dominant ideas, as the ideas of a dominant class, being imposed on subordinate classes is not tenable. They also show the manner in which the two doctrines which make up the conventional view of Marx's sociology of knowledge, relate to one another. The doctrine 'social being determines consciousness' tends to suggest that there are powerful reasons, chiefly class-interest, for supposing that each class will have its own distinctive system of belief. The 'base determines superstructure' doctrine, on the other hand, tends to argue that class-specific systems of belief become incorporated within a dominant ideology. The more that one stresses the significance of dominant ideas, the less easy is it to explain deviant, oppositional, or alternative beliefs. By showing the centrality of the concept of interest to conventional Marxist accounts and by suggesting that dominant ideas do not straightforwardly incorporate subordinate classes, I have been effectively arguing that conventional Marxist sociologies of knowledge stress the second doctrine to the neglect of the first.

Two particular points have been raised by the discussion so far and are in need of further elaboration. There is, firstly, the problem of relativism and, secondly, that of the relationship between Marxist sociology of knowledge and the method of analysis known as functionalism.

The Relativity of Beliefs

So far, I have been using the term 'ideology' in such a way that, in Marxism, the sociology of knowledge is more or less equivalent to the sociology of ideology. I have also suggested that ideology refers to beliefs that are in some sense distorted. The nature of ideology, and the precise sense in which it is distorted, are complex topics which will be treated more fully in Part II. However, at the least, it is clear that the quality of distortion has something to do with interest; to the extent that systems of belief are formed by interest, they are distorted. The conviction that class-interest distorts knowledge raises the problem of relativism, a problem that is endemic to the sociology of knowledge and which is often thought to be raised by *any* attempt to explain beliefs causally, and not just by those theories employing the concept of interest.

If all classes have class-interests, then all belief-systems must be distorted. It appears, therefore, that there are no criteria of truth and falsity (or distortion and non-distortion) that are independent of interest. Everything is relative, since everybody belongs to a class and has class-interests. This, incidentally, applies paradoxically to the doctrine that all interest-determined beliefs are distorted, as to all the propositions of Marxist theory. This can only be a disappointing result since Marxists plainly think of Marxism as a science which does reveal truth.

There are two main conventional solutions to this problem, both of which can be warranted from Marx's writings, which I will call the Doctrine of Proletarian Truth and the Doctrine of the Autonomous Science.

The Doctrine of Proletarian Truth accepts that, to the extent that beliefs are conditioned by class-interests, they are false. However, it suggests that it is not true, or will not be always true, that all social classes have a specific *class*-interest. Thus, at some point in history, the working class does not have class-interests, for its interests are the interests of the society as a whole. It is the harbinger of a new kind of society in which there are no social classes, hence no class-interest and hence no distortion of beliefs. The suggestion is that, so long as we know what the beliefs of the proletariat are, we can establish truth. There are several difficulties with this solution. Firstly, it is not clear at what point the proletariat stop having class-interests. It has plainly not happened yet, since it is widely conceded that the proletariat is still falsely conscious, a condition owed to the bourgeoisie's command over the 'means of mental production'. This means that somebody (possibly outside the proletariat) has to have a means of imputing a consciousness to the proletariat, of deciding what it would be if there were no false consciousness. Secondly, it is possible that the beliefs of members of the proletariat may actually contradict each other, and there will be no way of deciding between them, unless procedures can be introduced from outside. Thirdly, it seems unrealistic to speak as though there could be a society without competing social groups each of which will have conflicting interests (even if these are not class-interests).

The Doctrine of the Autonomous Science is, in many ways, the converse. It pretty well rejects the notion that classes can be without interests, but asserts that there is a branch of knowledge that can escape determination by class-interests and which develops autonomously outside the class structure. This doctrine implies a radical distinction between science and ideology. Ideologies are dominated by class-interest and are distorted, while science is interest free and true, or at least capable of providing methods which enable us to arrive at true propositions. The claim that science is an independent activity does seem a more promising solution to the problem than a conception which stresses the unique truth-bearing properties of a particular social group, but it carries with it its own difficulties. In particular, we have no ready-made criteria for distinguishing scientific from ideological knowledge. Furthermore it is very unsociological to suggest that science is divorced from all social practices and is not influenced by them. To sort out a Marxist conception of science, one must know in exactly what way science is to be seen as an autonomous practice.

Marxism and Functionalism

Functionalist methods of explanation are often supposed to be opposed to those of Marxism. They are thought to be static, to disregard conflict and perhaps worst of all, to be flawed by methodological difficulties in that they are not proper *causal* explanations. Similarly it is argued against functionalist theories of belief that they are circular or teleological. For example, a functionalist theorist, Apter,[27] argues that the function of socialist ideology in developing countries is to unite the nation behind a programme of development. In using a term like function, Apter has in mind the notion that social behaviour may have 'unintended effects'. Thus, it is not *necessary* that the leaders of under-developed countries should *intend* the propagation of socialist doctrine to act as a stimulus for social integration and development, only that it should in fact have that effect. Note that by the attribution of a function or effect, Apter is attempting an *explanation*. It is however, at first glance, an explanation of a peculiar kind. Diagrammatically we have:

Socialist ideology ⟶ integration ⟶ development.

Thus stated, this argument is not causally proper because the causal explanation of socialism is in terms of its effects; effects are placed before causes. However, arguments of this kind usually have an implicit premise which, in this case, could be of the form that social integration, in creating and sustaining a particular type of society, makes the continuation of socialism possible. Thus

Socialist ideology⟶ integration ⟶ development

kind of society which makes socialism
possible

The introduction of this other premise seems merely to exchange one problem for another, for the argument as a whole is circular. However, there is a further implicit premise, or, rather, the possibility of such a premise is not ruled out. This is that there is a first cause of socialism independent of the functional circle of socialism and development. This independent cause could be almost anything, say, the creation of a group of socialist intellectuals. The important point is that this is a kind of 'first cause' that sets the causal and functional relations between socialism and development going. Sociologically speaking, the first cause may be relatively unimportant, at least when compared with the continuing functional circle. In sum:

Socialist intellectuals⟶ socialism ⟶ integration ⟶ development

kind of society which makes socialism
possible.

Methodologically this argument is sound and it is functionalist in the sense that the functional circle is the prime object of sociological analysis. Construed in this way, the form of Apter's argument is remarkably similar to those of Marx, although, of course, the content is very different.

Earlier in this chapter I suggested that one of the central arguments of the conventional Marxist theory of belief was what could be called the 'ruling ideas model'. Since the dominant class have control of the means of mental production, they are able to impose their view of the world on the whole society. Ruling-class ideas are so pervasive throughout all levels of society through such media as the educational system, that subordinate classes literally do not have any other systems of belief available by means of which they might formulate their opposition. The adoption of the ruling ideas is thus one way in which subordinate classes are prevented from expressing political dissent or opposition. Pruning this argument down to its essentials one can say that the function of ('the effect of') the dominant ideology is to prevent the emergence of a revolutionary consciousness which in turn, through the mediation of other factors, ensures the continuation of the dominant ideology. Schematically the structure of the argument is the same as the ones I have already considered:

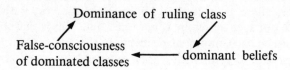

Again the argument looks circular. However in the Marxist scheme, circularity is avoided because the dominance of the ruling class is originally established by forces independent of the functional circle depicted above, firstly, by the domination of the particular mode of production, say capitalism, and ultimately, by the transformation, economic and political, that produced the domination of capitalism. For capitalist societies we have:

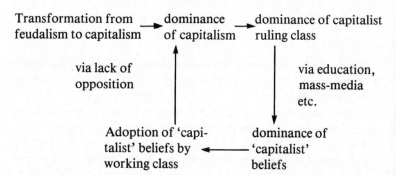

So far, I have argued that the ruling ideas model is functionalist in the sense discussed in the previous section, and that there is therefore nothing improper in the thesis from the strictly methodological point of view. I now have to examine another argument that is even more important to the conventional Marxist sociology of knowledge. When someone argues that a particular system of belief is formed by a particular class-interest, or is in the interests of a particular class, the relationship between belief and interest is a functional one. Inasmuch as these claims count as an explanation of the belief-system in question, the suggestion is that the belief has the effect of furthering interests, or that the function of the belief is a promotion of interests. Again, this argument does not seem to offend against any of the canons of acceptable explanation. That is to say, the explanation of the origins of the belief do not lie in the interests that it may continue to serve, although those interests may well explain its persistence. Thus, systems of beliefs may be initially formulated by groups of intellectuals or they may arise out of everyday experiences, but they may then come to serve particular interests. Nonetheless, this formulation of the logic of interest-explanations does conceal one interesting problem.

I have suggested that the initial cause of a system of belief may be unrelated to the factors that account for its persistence. However any satisfactory theory must still account for the *process* by which beliefs, originally almost 'accidentally' produced, come to serve particular class-interests. Such an account, in other words, must trace the history of a system of belief noting how it changes; it is rarely the case that a body of ideas springs into being as a perfect fit for class-interest. Various theories of the process are available. At one extreme it can be suggested that beliefs can be more or less consciously manipulated until they fit class-interest. At the other theoretical extreme it could be argued that there is a kind of evolution of belief-systems by which a process of natural selection winnows out elements of a belief-system because they do not meet any interest which would sustain them. The end product is a system of belief that persists because it furthers an interest.

Neither of these formulations is convincing. Conscious manipulation is rare, not the least because ideologists may not be very clear what class-interests actually are. The analogy with evolution in the animal kingdom is unsatisfactory precisely because changes in systems of belief are not 'natural'. The more likely possibility is that the expression, adoption, and change of beliefs takes place in a conceptual framework which is already heavily interest-determined and which limits the kinds of changes that are possible.

In this chapter I have been attempting to delineate the kinds of methods and theories employed within a conventional Marxist sociology of knowledge. Mannheim's sociology of knowledge, the subject of the next chapter, borrows heavily, but selectively, from this Marxist tradition.

---

2 MANNHEIM

If the conventional sociology of knowledge takes its inspiration from a particular interpretation of Marx, as described in the last chapter, that inspiration passes through a filter provided by Mannheim. Mannheim is often credited with being the founder of the sociology of knowledge. It certainly is true that his earlier writing is devoted to the justification of a sociological approach to knowledge, or rather to the assertion of its importance. However his work as a whole does present peculiar problems of interpretation. Above all, Mannheim did not regard himself as a systematic thinker. Quite the contrary, he thought that work that did aim principally at coherence might easily tend to suppress contradictions in the name of theoretical integrity. Underpinning this view is an epistemological position which sees reality as a confused mass of discrete items which cannot be theoretically represented in any tidy way, a conclusion particularly true of the 'fundamentally discordant character of our present situation'.[1] If reality does not *present itself* neatly, it cannot be *represented* neatly. Symptomatic of this view is Mannheim's tendency to see himself as an 'experimental thinker' and to present his work in an essay form. Even *Ideology and Utopia*, in its English edition perhaps the best-known of Mannheim's works, is in fact a collection of three essays written at different times, often expressing different opinions.

These tendencies indicate the importance of considering the *development* of Mannheim's views on the sociology of knowledge. It is often difficult to ascribe to him one unitary and coherent opinion on certain issues, particularly on the questions of relativism and the intellectuals, and injustice is often done by trying to do so.[2]

The Statement of the Problem

For Mannheim, the sociology of knowledge is an 'unmasking' enterprise which represents the 'systematization of the doubt' already present in everyday life. That is, to show that a person's thought is socially located, or socially determined, or a function of social position, is in some sense to go behind the face value of the thought itself to the social reality underneath. To do so is also to show that the thought is socially relative, partial, or distorted, in that it may be formed by particular social interests. However, the sociology of knowledge, which aims to reveal the social bases of thought, has to be distinguished from the everyday activity of unmasking particular assertions as more or less conscious deceptions motivated by self-interest. This distinction is presented by Mannheim as the distinction between total and particular ideology. Firstly, the particular conception of ideology calls into question only part of an opponent's assertions while the total conception doubts the whole world outlook and conceptual apparatus. Secondly, when one claims that an assertion is an example of a particular ideology, one is not denying that there are common standards of validity which would expose it as a deception. With total ideology however, the assumption is that the very criteria of truth are in doubt. Lastly, the particular conception operates with a vocabulary of interests, while the total ignores motivations, in 'confining itself to an objective description of the structural differences in minds operating in different social settings'.[3]

However, to analyse an opponent's position utilizing the total conception of ideology is not yet to perform an analysis in the sociology of knowledge. Another step is required which demands a further distinction between the special formulation of the total conception and its general formulation. The former applies the designation of total ideology only to the thought of an opponent, while the latter applies the designation to any body of thought. General ascriptions of total ideology are thus exercises in the sociology of knowledge. Given such a definition of his subject, Mannheim could hardly avoid giving a sociological account of the origins of the sociology of knowledge itself. Broadly, in periods of social stability and harmony, men can operate only with the particular conceptions of ideology since they all have a similar conceptual apparatus. In times of social conflict, however, men's social interests diverge and their systems of belief become irreconcilable. In these circumstances, men are pushed into explaining the beliefs of their opponents in terms of social factors like class or race. For Mannheim, the decisive conflicts were produced only in societies divided into classes, since it is only this form of social arrangement which produces irreconcilable antagonisms. Thus the sociology of knowledge is a comparatively modern form of intellectual enterprise, only appearing in a fully developed state in the nineteenth century.

Whatever the merits of Mannheim's historical account of the discipline, in this account he does not give us an adequate theoretical description of the general formulation of the total conception of ideology, which amounts to little more than a simple claim of the necessity of a *sociological* theory of thought. Thus, he will frequently assert the existence of a correlation between thought and social existence[4] or that 'not only do fundamental orientations, evaluations, and the content of ideas differ but that the manner of stating a problem, the sort of approach made, and even the categories in which experiences are subsumed, collected, and ordered vary according to the social position of the observer'.[5] The same point is made at some length, though in different terms, in the essay 'The Ideological and the Sociological Interpretations of Intellectual Phenomena'.[6] Mannheim here suggests that there are two ways of considering knowledge, which can be expressed in the distinction between 'ideal' and 'ideology'. 'In this sense, the intellectual phenomenon appears as idea in so far as it is considered "from within;" as ideology in so far as it is considered "from without" and is taken as the function of an "existence" posited outside of it . . .'.[7] The notions of idea and ideology both represent modes of interpretation of knowledge but they involve *fundamentally* different ways of considering the phenomenon. 'If I take, for instance, a theoretical statement simply as an idea, that is, "from within", I am making the same assumptions that are prescribed in it; if I take it as ideology, that is, look at it "from without", I am suspending, for a time, the whole complex of its assumptions, thus doing something other than what is prescribed in it at first glance.'[8] The sociology of ideas thus involves taking a quite special, extrinsic attitude to ideas. In turn, however, it is only one of several possible kinds of extrinsic interpretation of ideas, having the distinctive feature that it treats knowledge as a *function* of some other sphere, 'posited as real', such as 'civil society' or 'political economy'.

In very much the same spirit as the Marx of *The German Ideology*, Mannheim couples the necessity of a sociological account of ideas with denunciations of misconceptions. Thus the history of ideas, as a discipline, is condemned for its willingness to analyse changes in ideas in terms of 'epochs', a far too undifferentiated concept for the sociologist.[9] Followers of Hegel are blamed for promoting the thesis of the immanent evolution of ideas, 'a mirage of self-propelling ideas and a sublimated version of history narrated in a social vacuum'.[10] It is further mistaken to believe that it is the individual who thinks, for on the contrary, 'he thinks in the manner in which his group thinks', men think, 'in certain groups who have developed a particular style of thought'.[11]

The Construction of a System of Belief

Mannheim believes that analysis in the sociology of knowledge begins with the description of a system of belief, proceeds to an identification of the social group espousing that system of belief, and then shows what kind of relation exists between belief and social group. There is, right at the start of this procedure, a methodological problem which Mannheim recognized, but which has otherwise received relatively little attention from the sociology of knowledge.

The subject has to operate with some notion of a *system* of beliefs. This raises all sorts of questions. How, for example, does the analyst construct the system out of component beliefs, and what kind of relation is thought to hold between the separate beliefs? It is unusual to take the beliefs held by a single individual and refer to that as the system of belief appropriate to a social group. When the sociologist does discuss a system of belief, it is more generally one that is 'constructed' by the analyst and 'imputed' to the social group.

It is this process of construction that interests Mannheim in his essay 'On the Interpretation of Weltanschauung'.[12] He asks: 'What kind of task is a student of a cultural and historical discipline . . . faced with when he seeks to determine the global outlook (Weltanschauung) of an epoch. . . . Is the entity designated by the concept of Weltanschauung given to us at all, and if so—how is it given?'[13] Although Mannheim is apparently limiting himself to a particular kind of belief-system, namely Weltanschauung, he in fact understands that term in a fairly wide sense, and it is fair to say that his discussion applies to any manifestation of a belief-system.

The problem is, then, to show how it is that one can move from a consideration of the single item, be it belief, picture or poem, to the wider cultural totality or Weltanschauung. How does one deduce or construct the system from the individual propositions? Mannheim is clear that this cannot be through a simple addition of the individual items. Instead a new method is required, a 'mental operation transcending each objectification'. This method has to be a process of interpretation, a 'phenomenological analysis of the intentional acts directed towards cultural objects', and, more generally, an inspection of the *meaning* of cultural items.

As a preliminary exercise, Mannheim distinguishes three levels of meaning. Firstly, there is *objective meaning* which can be grasped by the observer without any knowledge of the intentions of the participants. 'All we need know is the "system" . . . that context and whole, in terms of which the data we perceive coalesce into a meaningful entity'.[14] By contrast, *subjective meaning* can be apprehended only 'from within' by a knowledge of the actor's intentions and purposes. *Documentary meaning* goes beyond both objective and expressive meaning; it refers to the meaning documented or indicated by a particular action, perhaps unintentionally. To illustrate the use of the three levels of meaning, Mannheim describes the action of a friend in giving alms to a beggar as he walks down the street. The objective meaning, deduced from the objective context of the act, is assistance. The subjective meaning, deduced from the friend's intentions, is, say, the attempt to convey a feeling of sympathy. However the observer may suddenly see his friend's action in a new light, say, as hypocrisy. This re-evaluation points beyond the act itself, for it involves taking a view of the whole character of the almsgiver as a hypocrite. Other manifestations of personality can be interpreted in the same way, all exhibiting a new stratum of meaning. 'Nothing will be interpreted in terms of consciously intended meaning, or in terms of objective performance; rather, every behavioural datum will serve to illustrate my synoptical appraisal of his personality as a whole.'[15] Just as documentary meaning can be applied to assessment of persons, so also does it apply to cultural items. As a commentator on Mannheim puts it: 'On the level of documentary meaning, interpretation points beyond the immediate behavioral or cultural data to a larger universe of facts which coalesce into a total personality configuration, or total socio-cultural context.'[16]

The concept of documentary meaning is the key to Mannheim's attempt at a solution to the problem of constructing systems of belief, for he believes that every cultural product has a documentary meaning which reflects a global outlook or Weltanschauung. The relation between items in a Weltanschauung or belief-system is simply that they all have the same documentary meaning. The analyst constructs a Weltanschauung by 'detaching certain elements or units of meaning from their concrete setting and fusing them into validly ascertainable objects of higher generality by using appropriate categories and conceptualisations'.[17] Unfortunately, this is as far as Mannheim goes, and his solution does not indicate how a common documentary meaning is detected or why a particular common theme is chosen so that the Weltanschauung presented is not arbitrary.

The Social Group as Base

So thought is, in some sense, a function of social group. When it comes to specifying what kind of social group, Mannheim is a kind of theoretical pluralist. The notion seems to be that the real world presents us with a vast diversity of social groups all of which have their own appropriate systems of belief, and theoretical schemes should represent this diversity. He does not approve of what he calls a onesideness which would see all thought as a function of one kind of group, say class. Thus:

By these groups we mean not merely classes, as a dogmatic type of Marxism would have it, but also generations, status groups, sects, occupational groups, schools, etc. Unless careful attention is paid to highly differentiated social groupings of this sort and to the corresponding differentiations in concepts, categories, and thought-models . . . it would be impossible to demonstrate that corresponding to the wealth of types of knowledge and perspectives which have appeared in the course of history there are similar differentiations in the substructure of society.[18]

For example Mannheim tries to indicate the sociological importance of the notion of generation which is 'one of the indispensable guides to an understanding of the structure of social and intellectual movements'.[19] A generation is not a group, association or organization, but a *social category* whose unity is constituted by a *similarity of location* of a number of individuals within a social whole. In this respect, generation is a concept similar to social class; both concepts refer to a similar location of a number of individuals in a social structure. Similarity of location can be defined only by identifying the social processes which generate the categories concerned. Thus:

> class position was based upon the existence of a changing economic and power structure. . . . Generation location is based on the existence of biological rhythm in human existence. . . . Individuals who belong to the same generation, who share the same year of birth, are endowed, to that extent, with a common location in the historical dimension of the social process.[20]

The crucial feature of common location is that it limits the range of experience open to an individual. It not only excludes certain possibilities, it also encourages the formation of 'certain definite modes of behaviour, feeling and thought'. The general theory of belief implicit in Mannheim's discussion of generation is, therefore, simply that common social location moulds men's ideas and different locations produce different ideas.

However Mannheim is careful to point out that generation groups may be internally stratified in a number of different ways and, in particular, by social class. Indeed, he insists that of all the social groups or locations that can be said to influence belief, 'class stratification is the most significant'.[21] Furthermore, in practice, in his *substantive* analyses he refers almost exclusively to class.

However, it is often not mainly classes considered statically that interest Mannheim, but the way that they may change their positions in an order of domination. Thus the beliefs appropriate to a class rising to dominance may be very different from those beliefs held by the very same class when it has achieved dominance. As Mannheim puts it, there is a distinction between ideology, which characterizes the belief-systems of dominant classes (or groups) and utopia, a pattern of thought appropriate to dominated classes (or groups). Thus:

> . . . ruling groups can in their thinking become so intensively interest-bound to a situation that they are simply no longer able to see certain facts which would undermine their sense of domination . . . in certain situations the collective unconscious of certain groups obscures the real condition of society both to itself and to others and thereby stabilizes it.
>
> The concept of utopian thinking reflects the opposite discovery of the political struggle, namely that certain oppressed groups are intellectually so strongly interested in the destruction and transformation of a given condition of society that they unwillingly see only those elements in the situation which tend to negate it . . . They are not at all concerned with what really exists; rather in their thinking they already seek to change the situation that exists.[22]

So, for Mannheim, ideology and utopia are both systems of belief 'incongruous' with reality. As such they are contrasted with 'situationally congruous' ideas, which are, perhaps unfortunately, all too rare.[23]

Ideologies may be inappropriate to reality, but they may also function to conceal it. Mannheim gives as an example the taboo against taking interest on loans. The rule that the lending of money should be carried on without the taking of interest is possible only in a world of 'intimate and neighbourly relations'. The more this world collapsed, the more the precept takes on an ideological character. Despite the fact that it is increasingly inappropriate, a dominant Church is able to use it as an ideological weapon against a rising capitalism.

The utopian mentality commands Mannheim's interest much more than does ideology. Utopias transcend reality rather than attempt to stabilize it. But because reality also changes, a particular brand of utopian thought can be caught up by a changing society and become the established doctrine. Although a particular utopia may thus no longer transcend reality, the utopian *mentality* persists for, in Mannheim's view, a new utopia arises. Thus, Mannheim is able to construct a history of the utopian mentality, which is marked by the sequence of the appearance and disappearance of particular utopias, starting with Chiliasm, working through Liberal–Humanitarianism and Conservatism and ending (so far) with Socialism–Communism. Mannheim's account of utopian thought is thus curiously Hegelian, in seeing the history of the utopian mentality as the history of an unchanging essence which is manifested in a series of particular utopias.

Perhaps the most crucial question about utopias is their relation to the dominant social order. Utopias are espoused by groups opposed to the dominant social order, by 'social strata struggling for ascendancy'.[24] Despite this political antagonism, Mannheim points out that it is almost impossible to formulate an idea of a utopia without making use of concepts borrowed from the dominant culture. However, even beyond this he indicates that there is a more organic, not to say mystical, connection between ideology and utopia. Thus:

> The relationship between utopia and the existing order turns out to be a 'dialectical' one. By this is meant that every age allows to arise (in differently located social groups) those ideas and values in which are contained in condensed form the unrealised and the unfulfilled tendencies which represent the needs of each age. These intellectual elements then become the explosive material for bursting the limits of the existing order. The existing order gives birth to utopias which in turn break the bonds of the existing order, leaving it free to develop in the direction of the next order of existence.[25]

In this passage, Mannheim again seems to be offering an idealist account of the historical relationship of ideology and utopia. The history of societies unfolds in a dialectic of opposing ideas which are based on the 'needs of each age'.

In sum, the point of the essay 'Ideology and Utopia' is to show that there is a distinctive set of ideas appropriate to dominant groups and an opposing set characteristic of ascendant groups and that the two are locked in continuing struggle. This is an abiding theme in Mannheim's work. In the essay 'Competition as a Cultural Phenomenon',[26] for example, he attempts to show that competition is a central feature of human societies, as if it were *intrinsic* to social order, perhaps derived from some features of human nature. In intellectual life competition is reflected in the desire for the imposition of an ideological hegemony: '. . . every historical, ideological, sociological piece of knowledge . . . is clearly rooted in and carried by the desire for power and recognition of particular social groups who want to make their interpretation of the world the universal one'.[27]

It will be clear that an important conclusion of Mannheim's work on ideology and utopia and competition is that the political struggle between groups is paramount. The fundamental cause of shifts in intellectual orientation is that struggle. Thus, Mannheim frequently uses the concept of class, *but* class is constituted by its place in political conflict, not by its place in a system of economic relations. Furthermore, he does not appear to have a convincing explanation of why it is that groups struggle.[28] Competition of this kind is simply a fact, or, is derived from the 'needs of the age'. Ideas, therefore, are not only political growths, they also have no visible roots.

Two further comments must be made. First, Mannheim does show that the position in an order of domination is a factor in the determination of the belief-system of a social group. This is an important point often neglected by conventional Marxist analyses, and I shall return to it in the next chapter. Secondly, Mannheim does *not* satisfactorily explain why, say, a particular dominant class will have particular ideas. Why, for example, does a feudal ruling class adopt the doctrines of Catholicism while a capitalist ruling class advocates classical liberalism?

The Connection between Thought and Social Existence

Even after one has constructed the system of belief in which one is interested and identified the social group to which that system is attached, there is still the problem of demonstrating the nature of the link between the two. At a sociological, rather than at an analytical level, this is the problem of showing how it is that the beliefs of social groups become articulated. For Mannheim, this articulation was the province of a special social stratum, the intelligentsia. As Heeren[29] points out, Mannheim changed his mind on this question several times in his career. In his first phase, he suggested that the way to do the sociology of knowledge was to indentify a particular world-view, identify the intellectual group espousing that view, and then to investigate the relationship between that group and the social classes. There was not necessarily a one-to-one relationship between a social class and an intellectual group. One social class might have several views, each of which was articulated by an intellectual group, or several classes might subscribe to the same view. Intellectuals would thus have considerable powers of expression, but in essence they *represented* the view of a class or classes. They were basically passive transmitters of class-interests. In this next, optimistic phase, intellectuals were seen as having their social origins in many different groups but they were regarded as beholden to none. This very diversity of social origin, together with the lack of social commitment, determined that intellectuals, as a group, could synthesize all the competing viewpoints represented in society into a harmonious whole. Intellectuals were, therefore, a positive force, if not *the* positive force, which might reconstruct a society the chief defect of which was anarchy—moral and intellectual.

Mannheim's optimism, was however, short-lived. Faced with the reality of European politics of the early 1930s, he began to see the social diversity of the intellectual stratum as a positive disadvantage, for this meant that intellectuals no longer formed a unitary group. Although the intelligentsia might be trained to see problems from every angle, individual intellectuals readily allied themselves with particular political forces in times of social stress. There was still a glimmer of hope, however, for intellectuals were likely to be *less* committed to one political view than non-intellectuals. In the last phase, Mannheim's interest had shifted away from the social attachments of intellectuals to the impact that mass society had on them. In his view, one of the most important functions of intellectuals was to preserve a society's culture and in mass society this function was endangered by the way in which the intellectual élite was democratized.

Although, as I have indicated, Mannheim took up various positions on the intellectual stratum, the one for which he is best known is that of the 'free-floating intelligentsia' capable of synthesizing many rival viewpoints. However, of more interest for his substantive exercises in the sociology of knowledge is the notion that the viewpoints of social classes and social groups do not present themselves automatically. On the contrary they require a specialized group of persons trained in particular ways. The difficulty is that the intellectual group will not always stand in the same relation to social classes. In some situations, at some times, intellectuals will be more independent of their related class, or classes, than at other times and consequently an analysis in the sociology of knowledge has to pay attention, not to the simple relation of thought to class, but to the complex interrelations between thought, intellectual group and class.

The mediating activities of intellectuals form one possible answer to the question of the *sociological* relationship between group and thought. However one must still pose this question on a theoretical level. I earlier suggested that Mannheim's theory of the relation of social group to thought was more or less a simple assertion that there was a connection between the two. We are not given much idea of the *mechanism* of the relation. In the previous chapter, I tried to show that Marxism did attempt to provide such a mechanism, that of class-interest, and, in doing so, advanced a theory concerning which beliefs did, *and* which did not, further class-interest. There are several reasons for demanding a specification of the mechanisms involved, but the most important is that, without it, one cannot know why a group should adopt one set of beliefs rather than another.

In fact, Mannheim does not ignore the notion of interest. It is, however, introduced into the discussion *ad hoc* and in an unexplained way. Thus, he often refers to the way that thinking arises out of the collective interests or purposes of the social group. However, when he does come to reflect *explicitly* on the role of interest in the determination of thought, he is usually critical of the use of the concept. His criticisms arise out of his dislike, noted earlier, of onesided or economic determinist arguments. He suggests that to employ the notion of interest exclusively in accounting for the correlation between thought and social group, is either to analyse only certain types of obviously interest-related beliefs or to define interest so widely that it loses all meaning. He continues:

> . . . the first thing to do is to overcome the one-sidedness of recognizing motivation by interest as the only form of social conditioning of ideas. This can be done most easily by a phenomenological demonstration of the fact that motivation by interest is merely one of many possible forms in which the adoption of certain attitudes by a psyche can be conditioned by social experience. Thus, it may be that we profess a certain economic theory or certain political ideas because they are in keeping with our interests. But surely no immediate interests are involved in our choice of a certain artistic style . . .[30]

Mannheim's suggestion that Marxism offers analysis only in terms of the pursuit of interest is an oversimplification. It is also crude to identify interest with *economic* aspiration, as it is to dismiss interpretation of artistic style in terms of interest. However, there is certainly a problem here. The version of Marxism that I presented in the previous chapter analysed beliefs either in terms of interest or in terms of a false consciousness induced by the bourgeoisie's command over the means of mental production. However, there may well be important systems of belief that are not analysable in either of these two ways, particularly those adopted by classes that were, but are no longer, dominant in society. These difficulties will be discussed in the next chapter.

Relativism

In general, Mannheim believes that any beliefs, or cultural products, can be analysed sociologically, everything that is, from political doctrines to artistic styles. However one of the most consistent points in his work is the view that mathematical, logical and scientific beliefs are exempt from social causation; these beliefs form an autonomous realm, governed by rules and procedures quite independent of social factors. Thus, in contrast to 'exisistentially determined thought' in 'mathematics and natural science, progress seems to be determined to a large extent by immanent factors, one question leading up to another with a purely logical necessity'.[31] Again, 'In the thought "$2 + 2 = 4$" there is no indication as to who did the thinking and where.'[32]

This distinction between two types of knowledge does not, on the face of it, seem very satisfactory. Among other things, it makes a sociology of science impossible in principle. However, Mannheim's discussion of the distinction is always tied up with another issue, namely relativism—a subject briefly discussed in the previous chapter. At one point, Mannheim says that the solution of the problem of relativism is the most important project in his sociology of knowledge. Despite the great deal of energy invested in the discussion of the subject however, he notoriously never arrived at a satisfactory solution. Indeed, his discussion is based on a misunderstanding of the implications of the social causation of ideas, a misunderstanding which in turn generates the unrealistic distinction between two types of knowledge.

There are three stages in the development of Mannheim's ideas about relativism. In the first stage, Mannheim very nearly accepts the implications of relativism. For him, knowledge is related to, or caused by, the social group reality. Each group has its own set of beliefs which cannot be compared with those of any other group. Further, Mannheim appears to believe that, to the extent that knowledge is caused in this way, it is false, distorted or partial. So for him, once the social determination of knowledge is established, the knowledge of one social group is as good as that of another and there are no independent criteria which would enable us to decide between rival knowledges. All knowledge is relative, a conclusion which makes the sociology of knowledge itself unreliable. There seems no way out of the vicious regress and apart from vague declarations of the need for a new 'dynamic' epistemology, Mannheim's only attempt at a solution is to suggest that there are categories of knowledge that are exempt from social causation.

In the second stage, Mannheim is no longer flirting with relativism. He is actively seeking a method of rejecting the apparent relativism implied by analyses in the sociology of knowledge and he aims to accomplish the rejection by the introduction of a new notion, that of relationism. Relationism applies only to certain kinds of knowledge; familiarly mathematical or scientific knowledge is exempted for they are (oddly) unrelated to the active purposes of mankind. Knowledge of the former kind has meaning only when it is related to a particular social and historical situation:

> A modern theory of knowledge which takes account of the relational as distinct from the merely relative character of all historical knowledge, must start with the assumption that there are spheres of thought in which it is impossible to conceive of absolute truth existing independently of the values and position of the subject and unrelated to the social context.[33]

Sociologists (and others) therefore have to give up all idea of independent criteria of validity or absolute truth. However, there is still the possibility of 'approximate truth' for 'knowledge arising out of our experience in actual life situations, though not absolute, is knowledge none the less'.[34] So Mannheim's position seems to be that existentially determined knowledge can only be partial, not absolute, and the thought of one social group or historical period cannot be compared with that of another. Mannheim's position here is notably unsound. He never elucidates the concept of absolute truth and, in any event, one could not tell if a body of knowledge is approximate without knowing what it is to which it approximates; one has to have the whole truth in order to know that someone else has only a part of it.

In later work, Mannheim modifies his concept of relationism, perhaps after the realization that the earlier formulation was an uneasy compromise. Here relationism often seems to be the same as the sociology of knowledge, in that systems of belief should be related to each other and to the social structure. For example, when a geographically mobile peasant boy thinks of his relatives 'he relates them to a certain mode of interpreting the world which, in turn, is ultimately related to a certain social structure which constitutes its situation. This is an instance of the "relational procedure".'[35] This modified doctrine of relationism has important implications for the relationship between epistemology and the sociology of belief, for Mannheim suggests that analysis of the origin of a proposition may make one *suspect* that it is only a partial view. Thus it is true that ultimately there is no substitute for 'a direct examination of the facts'. However it may also be plain from the circumstances in which an argument is advanced that it is distorted, since 'A position in the social structure carries with it the probability that he who occupies it will think in a certain way.'[36] Thus, Mannheim has effectively abandoned the notion that social circumstances determine truth-value, though without believing that they have nothing to do with truth.

This last position is altogether more coherent than the earlier versions, and it paves the way for the transformation of the problem of relativism engineered in the third stage of Mannheim's work. In this stage, Mannheim believes that the important difficulty raised by the sociology of knowledge is the revelation that men's judgements are distorted by their *values*. The only way to control values is to bring them into the open so that in seeing their values, men may overcome them. It is therefore no longer the technical difficulty of evading a paradoxical relativism, but a practical one of disentangling the values and interests which may colour perceptions and judgements.

One of the striking things about Mannheim's discussion of relativism is its 'fundamental indecision'. In some ways this is a systematic indecision generated by a mistaken view of the implications of having a causal theory of belief. Thus Mannheim seems to have believed, at least in his earlier work, that to say of a belief that it is causally related to social structure is to say that it is false or partial. Given this premise, it is not surprising that Mannheim got involved in a relativistic tangle. As I have already indicated, Mannheim himself appeared to relax this premise in his later work, by suggesting that a demonstration of the social causes of a belief might make one merely *suspect* its partiality.

Conservative Thought

Mannheim was at his best when dealing with substantive material and some of these empirical exercises are excellent examples of the methods of the sociology of knowledge. The best of all is the essay,

'Conservative Thought', which is often cited by Mannheim as *the* example of his method.

Mannheim believes that conservative thought is a very specific *style* of thought, an 'objective mental structure', which occurred at a particular time in a particular social situation. Since the field is a rather broad one he chooses to study in detail certain thinkers in Germany in the earlier part of the nineteenth century. His method of presentation, which to some extent anticipates Merton's paradigm,[37] is first to delimit the components which make up conservative thought, and then to show how this thought is related to a social base.

Firstly, conservative thought must be distinguished from thinking that is merely traditional. 'Traditionalism signifies a tendency to cling to vegetative patterns, to old ways of life which we may well consider as fairly ubiquitous and universal.'[38] Conservative thought, however, is not to be understood in 'some general psychological sense', but as a particular mode of thought related to 'a concrete set of circumstances'. For Mannheim, all modes of thought consist of a 'basic intention' which represents the most basic assumptions shared by all who think in the specified manner, and also a set of key 'problems' which represents the theoretical components worked out by the more intellectual spokesmen. In the case of German conservative thought, the basic intention has five main elements, namely:

> its emphasis on concreteness as against abstractness; its acceptance of enduring actuality, as compared with the progressive desire for change; the illusory simultaneity it imparts to historical happenings as compared with the liberal linear conception of historical development; its attempt to substitute landed property for the individual as the basis of history; and its preference for organic social units rather than the agglomerative units such as "classes" favoured by its opponents.[39]

The abstract key problem of conservative thought is an opposition to natural-law thought,[40] an opposition both methodological and substantive.

It may be seen from the brief description of conservative thought given above that Mannheim cannot describe the style without presenting it as *opposing* something. Thus, conservative thought takes a great deal of its impetus from opposition to other ideas common in the eighteenth and early nineteenth centuries. In particular, it opposes the system of thought that Mannheim calls rationalism. Rationalism is interested in quantification and calculation. It does not want to know more about things than can be 'expressed in a universally valid and demonstratable form'. It is thus interested in generalities not particulars and 'appreciates in man only that which "generalises" . . . that is to say, Reason'.[41] Rationalism is a style of thought informing many fields of knowledge and activity especially natural science and economic behaviour.

For Mannheim, rationalism is very closely bound up with a particular social group:

> as to the sociological factor which accounts for the growth of this consistent rationalism, the common view is no doubt correct, that it is the rising capitalist bourgeoisie . . . it is not that every individual bourgeois approached the world in this way continuously and at all times, but merely that the social aims of the bourgeoisie as the propagators of capitalism made such a consistently abstract and calculating form of experience possible.[42]

Conservative thought, then, is in self-conscious opposition to rationalism which is the mode of thought characteristic of the capitalist bourgeoisie. The crucial point that Mannheim now has to settle concerns the social base of conservative thought. Which social groups espouse conservative thought, and why?

It will be remembered that, when approaching a sociological analysis of a style of thought, Mannheim believes that one must consider both the intellectual spokesmen and the social groups for which the intellectuals speak. In Mannheim's view, the 'unattached intellectuals' of early nineteenth-century Germany became the spokesmen of conservative thought primarily because they had no other means of support. They became 'mercenary pamphleteers', ready to use their skills in the service of any cause. Mannheim is very clear in this work that the intelligentsia have no interests of their own:

their own social position does not bind them to any cause, but they have an extraordinarily refined sense for all the political and social currents around them, and the ability to detect them and enter into their spirit. By themselves they know nothing. But let them take up and identify themselves with someone else's interests—they will know them better, really better, than those for whom these interests are laid down by the nature of things, by their social condition.[43]

Intellectuals thus act as spokesmen for the interests of groups unable to express those interests themselves. So, what groups are going to have the interests that require legitimation in the form of conservative thought? Mannheim suggests that it is those groups outside the 'capitalistic process of rationalization' that is 'the peasant strata, the petit-bourgeois groups which had descended directly from the handicraftsmen of earlier times and the aristocratic tradition of the nobility'.[44] Perhaps more accurately this is an alliance between groups genuinely outside capitalism, the peasantry and petit-bourgeoisie, and those supplanted by capitalism, particularly the nobility. It is especially the latter on which Mannheim concentrates, for in his view it is from a class beginning to be displaced as the ruling class that one might expect the most fervent opposition. Further, the nobility was in the best position to support intellectual spokesmen.

Conservative thought thus comes from groups in opposition to capitalism, and it is this that gives the oppositional quality to the ideas of conservative intellectuals. Indeed Mannheim often gives the impression that conservative thought is simply a convenient ideological weapon picked up by the nobility already engaged in political, economic and social conflict with capitalism. Any set of ideas would do as long as it controverted the claims of bourgeois rationalism. However, ideologies are not simply debating weapons; as well as opposing the ideas of other groups, they match, in some sense, the 'life experiences' of the groups espousing them. For example, Mannheim suggests that the categories of bourgeois thought are formed in the way they are because they further the political and economic *interests* of the bourgeoisie. The bourgeoisie did not 'choose' the ideas of the Enlightenment at random: these *particular* ideas formed in response to *particular* interests. One ought therefore to pose similar questions with respect to conservative thought. Why did the nobility take up these *particular* ideas and not others? Unfortunately, Mannheim does not give an adequate answer to this question. It is not that conservative thought matches the nobility's interests, at least not in the same (economic) sense that rationalism matches the interests of the bourgeoisie. *Some* elements of conservative thought, the moral importance of the *status quo* for example, might well suit the political interests of a *dominant* class, and it would be possible to say that the nobility were at least politically dominant in the first half of the nineteenth century in Germany. Mannheim gives another kind of interpretation when he suggests that the intellectuals, in forming nineteenth-century conservative thought, were rediscovering feudal–romantic ideas which had been submerged for some considerable length of time. This interpretation merely raises the problem in a fresh guise, for we still have to ask why this particular system of belief was recovered. This notion of some kind of continuation of conservative ideas over a long period of time also appears to contradict Mannheim's assertion that conservative thought was something new which could have arisen only in particular social circumstances. In sum, Mannheim is very successful in establishing a *correlation* between conservative thought and the existence of certain social groups, but his explanation of the correlation is incomplete. We know that conservatism appealed to the nobility and the intellectuals because it opposed the categories of bourgeois rationalism, but the further question, 'why *those* ideas and not some other oppositional set', is left largely unanswered.

Mannheim, Marx and the Conventional Position

It is often said that Mannheim was the founder of the sociology of knowledge. It is also often said that he was a Marxist. Both these claims are partly true and partly false. Mannheim did think that he was borrowing, or adapting, some of his central concepts from Marx and, inasmuch as the conventional position takes its inspiration largely from Mannheim, it is also influenced by Marx.

However, the implication of the discussion in this chapter is that

Mannheim's Marxism is a special interpretation of Marx. This, in turn, has given the sociology of knowledge a particular cast, some of whose features are criticized in Part II.

There are three closely connected respects in which Mannheim's borrowings from Marx are suspect. First, it often appears from commentaries[45] that the outstanding feature that makes Mannheim's work Marxist is his employment of the concept of class. In fact, Mannheim really offers an account of social *groups* based on the central, but vague, concept of 'similarity of location'. However, there is a theoretical arbitrariness here, for Mannheim has no theory which enables him to relate these groups to one another or to other features of society; he simply offers a list of groups and their attendant systems of belief. Marx, on the other hand, locates class in a general theory of political economy; this is, at least, a theoretical scheme which provides explanations of surface phenomena and enables one to judge the relative importance of the elements in the scheme.

It is perhaps a little unfair to suggest that there is no theory underlying Mannheim's list of social groups, for he suggests at various points in his work that social classes are constituted by their place in a *political* struggle. This struggle for domination between classes (and other social groups) is seen as endemic to human society; history is considered as a rising and falling of groups in political dominance. Again, however, this is an incomplete account, for there is no explanation of the struggle itself. Such an explanation is however provided by Marxism in its insistence on the importance of the economy. In the crucial respect of emphasizing questions of competition and domination to the neglect of the economy, he is only eccentrically a Marxist.

Thirdly, there is a kind of implicit epistemology underlying Mannheim's more specific propositions. Throughout his work he insistently argues against 'systematic' thinking or 'one-sided' demonstration. Curiously, given Mannheim's intellectual origins, these dislikes push him into what could be called a 'naive empiricism', in which the importance of theory is devalued. Of course, it is true that he gave often very convincing explanations of particular systems of belief, such as conservatism or utopia, but these explanations are not offered from within a more general social theory. One of the consequences is the kind of arbitrariness mentioned earlier. Now, whatever the merits of such an epistemology, it is certainly not Marxist,[46] for not only does Marx insist on the importance of prior theoretical construction, he also offers a general social theory.

It is tempting to be dismissive of Mannheim's work, and to some extent I have fallen to this temptation. In essence, the criticisms that I have made of him derive from his method of working, from his tendency to pick up a problem but then not to follow through its implications or to recognize its theoretical difficulties. However, one must also recognize that Mannheim has been immensely influential. This reputation is not totally undeserved for, just as he was not a systematic thinker, he was capable of recognizing interesting problems and of providing brilliant insights. These qualities of mind make him a source of inspiration rather than of solutions. His influence has another origin however. I have argued that he borrowed selectively from Marx. This borrowing was not restricted to Mannheim, or even to the sociology of knowledge. Quite the contrary, Mannheim's image of Marx matches up very well with that image characteristic in other branches of sociology. Mannheim is influential at least partly because his work is so consistent with the approach of sociology as a whole.

---

3 SOME DIFFICULTIES IN THE CONVENTIONAL POSITION

I suggested in the Introduction to this book that there is a 'conventional' position in the sociology of knowledge and it is a variant of this position that I have been describing in the previous two chapters. The main features of this position are as follows:

(1) One can identify systems of belief which are in some sense supra-individual. Thus, not only do individual beliefs 'hang together', but they are also shared between individual members of a society in such a way that it is possible that no one individual holds all the beliefs that make up a system. The claim that *systems* of belief can be identified in this way is often indicated in the use of such terms as 'outlook', 'perspective', or 'world-view' to describe the beliefs of some social group.

(2) The explanation of the sharing of systems of belief must be *social*. Both Marx and Mannheim spent a good deal of time

rejecting non-social explanations, as is instanced in their common dislike of Hegel's work. Of course, in a sense, this principle is nothing more than a definition of the sociology of knowledge. Thus most writers in the subject would agree with Macquet that 'we may define the sociology of knowledge as the study of mental productions as related to social or cultural factors'.[1] Nonetheless it has historically been important to *assert* the principle, to establish the subject as a proper area of inquiry.

(3) The focus of investigation is the social group, or social location, in Mannheim's terms. It is the social group that provides the directed environment in which the beliefs are learnt and this is the reason that particular sets of beliefs are 'appropriate' to particular social groups. The kinds of group (or social process) involved may be very diverse, as Merton indicates in the following list: 'social position, class, generation, occupational role, mode of production, group structures (University bureaucracy, academics, sects, political parties), "historical situation", interests, society, ethnic affiliation, social mobility, power structure, social processes (competition, conflict, etc.).'[2] The notion that every definable social location has at least the theoretical possibility of having a particular belief-system that is appropriate to it is the most important tenet of the conventional sociology of knowledge. It is also the source of a weakness, for the *correlation* of a system of belief with a social location does not necessarily *explain* why *that* location should produce, or be associated with, *that* particular form of belief.

(4) Of all possible social groups, social class is one of the most important in the formation of belief. As Gurvitch argues: 'there is no doubt that social classes, to the extent that they exist, are in mutual conflict; now these conflicts . . . have a strong influence upon states and churches, and other specific groups. It is this which would seem to justify the Marxist thesis that in the area of the sociology of knowledge, social classes are much more important sources than the specific groups.' However Gurvitch adds, as Mannheim could well have done: 'But we must guard against the temptation to be dogmatic.'[3] Social classes are important but they are not of final importance. Even Scheler, certainly no Marxist, was at pains to emphasize the differences in outlook that obtain between classes.[4]

(5) The causal mechanism correcting class to belief is 'interest'. As I have indicated, although this concept is of great importance to the sociology of knowledge, it is not used in a clear and straightforward manner. Conventional Marxist accounts tend to take it for granted, while Mannheim both relied on it and criticized its 'one-sided' use in Marxism. For other writers, interest is thought to be too restrictive a notion that does not make a great deal of sense of the relation between belief and social locations other than class.

(6) The conception of societies as constituted by opposed social classes is associated with the notion that, generally, societies are dominated socially, politically, and economically, by particular social classes. In Marxism, this view gives rise to the 'ruling ideas' model, and, in Mannheim, it informs the distinction between ideology and utopia.

There are, of course, accounts of the sociology of knowledge that do not fit this scheme. Sorokin, for example, analyses particular forms of knowledge by relating them to 'culture mentalities' which are themselves forms of thought, albeit fundamental ones.[5] Again, there are variations within the position that I have described (from 'left' to 'right'). These variations are determined by the degree to which writers hold that class is important and that knowledge is *determined* by social structure, rather than produced by unconstrained individuals. Nonetheless, these divergencies do not represent significant differences of method, only of emphasis. In this light, one may take Mannheim as a fair representative of the conventional position in the sociology of knowledge and he certainly occupies the dominant position in the subject.

In this chapter, I want to illustrate the advantages of the conventional position by trying to show how it can make sense of the concept of individualism. This illustration also shows up some of the weaknesses of the method, and I shall conclude with an examination of some of these weaknesses from the point of view of the two alternative approaches briefly outlined in the Introduction.

Individualism

Every social theory has to have a conception of the individual and his place in relation to other social entities or supra-individual entities. Indeed such theories may be differentiated from one another on the basis of their particular views of the individual. However, there is one set of social theories whose distinguishing feature is the insistence on the social priority of the individual *vis-à-vis* the State, the established Church, social classes, or other social classes, or other social groups. Such doctrines are often said to express an *individualism*.[6]

The notion of individualism is pervasive throughout Western social and political thought. Thus one finds apparently similar notions employed in political and economic theory, religious doctrine, discourses on morality, and even in literature. Not only is there an intellectual heterogeneity, there is also a temporal diffusion. Thus, the heyday of political individualism in England is often said to be the seventeenth and early eighteenth centuries, while religious individualism is to be found much earlier and economic individualism rather later. However, the notion is probably best known for its connection with classical liberalism in the two centuries 1650–1850. Thus as Manning observes, in its earlier phases, from Locke to Mill, 'liberalism treats the individual as prior to society as a historical being or philosophical concept. Many liberals assert that society is not more than the sum total of its members whose rights or interests its institutions are properly concerned to protect'.[7] The prime object of sociological investigation is therefore a 'classical' period of individualistic thought predominant in the seventeenth, eighteenth and early nineteenth centuries.

The conventional sociological theory is that, despite the apparent diffusion of conceptions of individualism, the doctrine as a whole is related in some way or other to the appearance or dominance of capitalism. For example, Goldmann[8] is interested in providing a sociological explanation of the basic categories of Enlightenment thought. He believes that there are seven such categories: the autonomy of the individual, contract, equality, universality, toleration, freedom and property. The most important of these is the first, which is so basic that it 'offers a direct means of making the intellectual history of the western European bourgeoisie comprehensible'.[9] Underlying Enlightenment thought was a conception of the individual as 'a sort of moral point of departure'. Society is seen as resulting from the 'action of countless autonomous individuals on each other and in response to each other, behaving as rationally as possible for the protection of their private interests and basing their actions on their knowledge of the market with no regard for any trans-individual authority or values'.[10] It is the same individualism that underpins the 'two great world visions characteristic of the European outlook', empiricism and rationalism, and also their synthesis in the French Enlightenment, despite their apparent considerable dissimilarities. All these systems of thought have, as a common assumption, the notion that the individual consciousness is the absolute origin of all knowledge.

Goldman relates the development of individualism, and all the other categories of Englightenment thought, to the development of a particular economy, the capitalist or bourgeois economy in which the crucial feature is the prominence of well-developed markets for goods and services. This feature he derives in turn from Marx's analysis of the commodity form in *Capital*. Thus a distinctive feature of capitalism is that goods are not produced for direct use, but for their exchange-value. An economy dependent on the exchange-value of goods produced requires markets in which the exchange-value can be realized.

All the Enlightenment categories are related to the necessity of such markets. For example, parties to an exchange must be able to respect each other's title to the goods that they exchange; there must, in other words, be a law of private property. Similarly, free markets demand that there be no impediment to exchange from religious or moral considerations; there must be religious toleration. Most important of all, however, is the manner in which markets demand individualism. The basic assumption of exchange is the view that 'every individual appears as the autonomous source of his decisions and actions'.[11] *Individuals* are recognized as free, equal and autonomous agents entering into unfettered contracts to exchange. MacPherson, in his study of seventeenth-century English political theory, offers a similar account, although it is perhaps less sociologically precise. He suggests that seventeenth-century political theory is informed by one crucial assumption: that of possessive individualism. This is the assertion that 'every man is naturally the sole proprietor of his own person and capacities (the absolute proprietor in the sense that he owes nothing to society for them) and especially the absolute proprietor of his capacity to labour. Every man is therefore free to alienate his own capacity to labour.'[12] The assumption of possessive individualism was what gave liberal theory its power for it 'did correspond to the reality of seventeenth century market society'.[13] A theory that depicts society as essentially a set of relations of exchange between individual proprietors each of whom owns his own capacities, will be effective in a society dominated by markets in which such exchanges really do happen. It is not so effective, MacPherson argues, in contemporary society, where reality does not match theory so closely.

Individualism and the Novel Form

So far, I have attempted to identify a concept of individualism and to provide arguments linking that concept to the appearance of capitalist society. I now want to illustrate the discussion of individualism in greater detail in a more specialized context, that of the appearance of the novel form in England in the second half of the eighteenth century.

It has been argued, most importantly by Watt,[14] that the novel, as it developed in the hands of Defoe, Fielding and Richardson, represented a decisive break with literary tradition; it was, literally, a novel form. It was also a *form* the central concerns of which were closely connected with the intellectual climate of the day. The novel had two closely connected characteristics, individualism and realism. The former is mostly represented as a kind of particularization, a stress on the particular rather than the general, while the latter denotes a belief in the 'individual apprehension of reality through the senses'. For Watt, then, the novel, or rather the novels of these three authors, were defined by the combination of these two traits. The essence of the novel is 'truth to individual experience—individual experience which is always unique and therefore new';[15] from the Renaissance onwards 'there was a growing tendency for individual experience to replace collective tradition as the ultimate arbiter of reality'.[16]

A number of technical characteristics of the novel contribute to a story which claims to be a plausible description of the actual experiences of individuals. For example, Defoe and Richardson departed from the literary conventions of their day in not using mythology, legend or history as the basis of the plot. Traditional plots were accepted because they rested on the assumption prevalent in all areas of intellectual life at the time, that nature and man were unchanging. Defoe, however, allowed his plots to develop from his own sense of what his characters 'might plausibly do next'. 'In so doing Defoe initiated an important new tendency in fiction: his total subordination of the plot to the pattern of the autobiographical memoir is as defiant an assertion of the primacy of individual experience in the novel as Descartes' "Cogito ergo sum" was in philosophy.'[17]

Plots like those of Defoe had also to have a new sense of character. While traditional plots took general human types as central characters, in the new convention *particular* people acted out the plot in particular circumstances. This particularization of character is shown in the technique of naming characters. In the older convention characters often had names denoting general human qualities. A name like Robinson Crusoe, however, indicates a particular person. Indeed, the tradition of giving realistic names is now so well established that *not* to do so is to run the risk of destroying the reader's belief in the credibility of the character.

Particularization of time and space also became significant for the novel, and the accurate description of the passage of time is important for the structure of the plot. Causally important events in the story are placed in a sequence instead of being timeless or included in an artificial twenty-four-hour period. *Robinson Crusoe*, for example is set in a particular time, and the passage of time is a noticeable feature of the novel's progress. Similarly, location in space is important for Defoe, Richardson and Fielding. It is not just that the action of the novel takes place in definable places. It is also that the reader is given a strong impression of place by the often exhaustive description of objects or buildings in the physical environment.

The net effect of the eighteenth-century novel's departure from the prevailing literary conventions is to emphasize the *reality* of *individual* experience. The novel incorporates a world-vision which 'presents us, essentially, with a developing but unplanned aggregate of particular individuals having particular experiences at particular times and at particular places'.[18]

Defoe's *Robinson Crusoe* is often supposed to be the classical literary statement of individualism. Its plot is frequently referred to by both admirers and detractors, in such terms as to make it an archetypal myth of capitalist society.[19] Besides the technical characteristics of the novel form noted above, a number of features of the plot of *Robinson Crusoe* contribute to making it a celebration of individualistic virtues. Perhaps most important is the view of the central character as hero. Crusoe acts as an individual. His moral choices are his own; he is not fettered by custom or tradition. Indeed, Defoe pictures him as an emotional isolate. He can sell his friends, and his relationships with women are strictly instrumental, since they are useful either as labourers or as providers of capital. Further, Crusoe is an *active* hero, for he actively seeks to transform the world around him to fit in with his individual interests, and the isolation of the island existence provides a device for the demonstration of the pursuit of individual advancement. These qualities of technique and plot point to the essential individualism of the novel. However what makes the story a characteristic myth of capitalist society is not the individualism *per se*, but its association with other features, such as the emphasis on the virtues of work; the vices of unproductive leisure; the exploitation of natural resources; and the pursuit and accumulation of capital.[20]

Individualism as Dissent

Watt's work provides us with a good understanding of what kind of individualism is at work in the eighteenth-century novel. Unfortunately, as far as sociologises are concerned, he is rather less precise about the relationship of the ideas that he discusses to parallel social developments. Thus, he suggests that the novel's 'serious concern with the daily lives of ordinary people' will depend on the existence of a society which considers the individual to be a valuable object of study. The existence of such a society, in turn, obviously depends on a special type of economic and political organization and on an appropriate ideology; more specifically on an economic and political organization 'which allows its members a very wide range of choices in their actions, and an ideology based, not on the tradition of the past, but on the autonomy of the individual, irrespective of his particular social status or personal capacity'.[21] Watt cites two causes of this dramatic social change: the rise of industrial capitalism on the one hand, and the spread of certain varieties of Protestant religious belief on the other. It is not clear whether the social changes produced the novel form or if the literary change had some other source. Again, the economic history is vague in that 'industrial capitalism' is too undifferentiated a concept. Goldmann is similarly ambiguous about the precise relationship between individualism and capitalism. At times, he talks of systems of belief as being a consequence of economic changes, and, at others, of their being a *precondition* of the establishment of a new mode of production. He can also resort to the vaguer formulation that the structure of Enlightenment thought is 'analogous' to the structure of the market economy. These theoretical ambiguities point to problems general in any attempt at establishing a correlation between individualism and capitalism.[22] Not only is there an enormous time scale over which individualist doctrines are said to have appeared, capitalism is often presented as a unitary social phenomenon with the same relationship to systems of belief at every stage of its development.

Implicit in many of the sociological accounts, not only of individualism but more generally of seventeenth, eighteenth and nineteenth century political, economic and social thought, there is a theory of the relationship of belief to economy very like that discussed in Part I(1). Individualist beliefs are articulated by an intellectual stratum that is attached to a social class, namely the rising capitalist class. The beliefs serve the interests of that class because they fit with the economic workings of capitalism in the sense that capitalism *requires* that persons are treated as free and equal independent economic units able to buy and sell in unrestricted markets. Whatever the origins of the various doctrines of individualism (see pp. 28–32), they will help to meet that requirement.

A partial explanation (though still with some defects) of the appearance of doctrines of individualism is therefore couched in terms of the *interests* of a social class which is itself embedded in a particular mode of production. However there is another, equally attractive, interpretation. Individualistic doctrines, in that their essence is a freedom for the individual from the constraints of tradition, custom and society, effectively permit or encourage *dissent* from the prevailing social arrangements. In such doctrines, it is not only the right of individuals to make their own moral and political decisions, it is their positive duty. Individualism, therefore, might be taken up by groups of any kind which oppose the *status quo* and require ideological legitimation of their dissent. On this view, the kind of individualism that I have been discussing is not so much in the economic interests of a capitalist class, but instead serves the political needs of the moment; individualism is not tied to capitalism as such, but only to capitalism in a particular phase of its relation with other, dominant, modes of production. In general, this suggests that beliefs will vary with the position of a class in order of domination rather than with economic interests specific to a mode of production. Individualism is appropriate to simple opposition.

To some extent, this interpretation is supported by a consideration of the later history of doctrines of individualism, for it seems that individualism is characteristic of the earlier phases of capitalism rather than of the later. As Manning observes:

> it has frequently been observed that in its earlier phases, liberalism treats the individual as prior to society as an historical being or philosophical concept. Many liberals assert that society is not more than the sum total of its members whose rights or interests its institutions are properly concerned to protect. It is claimed that it does not evolve over time. . . . In later liberal thought the subservience of society to man is a muted theme and the idea that it does not evolve is no longer heard. [23]

When the capitalist class in England in the seventeenth and early eighteenth centuries was in political and economic opposition to a dominant feudal ruling class, individualism was a lively and dissenting set of beliefs. When capitalism became dominant, however, the assertion of the importance of the individual became less strident, as there became less need for capitalism to counter other social forces in society. As Goldmann suggests:

> The individualist view possesses content only in certain his-

torical situations; it did so most notably in the eighteenth century, but it can still do so now, whenever its basic values (freedom, equality, toleration, etc.) are in danger and need to be defended; however when these values are dominant in society and not directly faced with any serious threat, individualism tends to revert to its purely formal character and lose the power of giving meaning to human life. [24]

However, Goldmann's view rather oversimplifies the picture. It is not only the case that individualist doctrines become less strident as capitalism becomes established. It is also true that in late nineteenth and twentieth century political theory and practice individualism comes to be seen as a source of social problems rather than moral virtues. Conceptions of the primacy of the individual become *replaced* by doctrines which emphasize the obligations of the individual to the social whole. [25]

So far, I have suggested that there are two interpretations of the relationship of individualism to capitalism. The more orthodox one (the 'interest explanation') suggests that individualism suits the interests of a capitalist class in its specific economic practice. The second interpretation (the 'dominance explanation') claims that individualism has little to do with economic interests and much more to do with the necessity of the legitimation of dissent. The relationship between these two explanations is only partly touched on in the conventional sociology of knowledge outlined in previous chapters. Mannheim did see the importance of the position of a class in an order of domination in his distinction between ideology and utopia. Ideologies, it will be remembered, are those systems of belief justifying the *status quo* and favoured by dominant groups. Utopias, on the other hand, inasmuch as they oppose the dominant classes, represent the beliefs of classes attempting to impose *their* social order. Marx also made a few comments on the subject. For example in *The German Ideology*, he distinguishes between theories corresponding to the 'struggling, still underdeveloped bourgeoisie', and those appropriate to 'the ruling, developed bourgeoise'. [26] A contemporary Marxist, Williams, in re-examining the concept of base and superstructure, points to the importance of considering oppositional and alternative, as well as dominant, cultures. [27] These comments could be developed into a theory the

central insistence of which is that interests cannot be conceived of
either as static, or as operating in a vacuum. On the contrary,
interests will change as a class gains or loses dominance and will
vary with changing relationships with other classes. As these interests change, so also will the systems of belief, and it might be
possible to write a kind of history of the changes in belief-systems
as the appropriate classes rise, become established, and decline in
political and economic power.[28]

Both the interest and dominance explanations are plausible and,
in fact, there is no reason to see them as contradictory. It could be
simultaneously the case that individualism suits the interests of the
capitalist class *and* that it legitimates the dissent of that class in an
early stage of its development. Such an accommodation between
the two interpretations provides an overall sociological, account of
individualism which follows the main tenets of the conventional
sociology of knowledge sketched out at the beginning of this
chapter. It is an account which still has its theoretical problems,
however. First, it looks as if it were pure accident that individualism both 'fitted' the workings of the capitalist economy
and legitimated the dissent of a capitalist class. Secondly, we are
not told how a capitalism which, in its origin, to some extent
depended on beliefs like individualism, could work perfectly well in
its later phases without those beliefs. I shall argue in the next
section of the book that a partial answer to these questions rests in
an analysis of the concept of the mode of production as a
mechanism which explains *both* the economic workings of
capitalism *and* the necessity of a political struggle between classes
with class-interests.

I have argued so far that the conventional sociology of
knowledge can provide an initially plausible, though not complete,
interpretation of individualistic doctrines. I turn now to a brief
consideration of another set of doctrines which is not so easily
explained.

Conservatism

It is unfortunate that sociologists of knowledge have concentrated
so much on 'bourgeois' thought, for their attention has been

diverted away from consideration of equally important systems of belief like conservatism. By conservative thought, I mean neither the principles that underlie the practice of the Conservative Party, nor common-sense habitual or traditional thinking. Conservative theoreticians often repudiate attempts to define conservatism, claiming that it does not represent any coherent body of doctrine. Doubtless it is always dangerous to try to cram writers of apparently diverse persuasions into rigid moulds of any kind. Nonetheless, there are good reasons for suggesting that at least since the early nineteenth century in Europe and arguably much earlier, there has been a distinctive stream of conservative thought, consisting of a description of certain features of society, a causal explanation of those features (a diagnosis) and a prescription of the measures necessary to remedy any faults. For conservatives, society, or more particularly, capitalist society, has a number of closely connected defects. Chief among these is the anarchy and disorder of social relations. Secondly, there is a conception of society as a mass-society where people are like atoms. This in turn has the effect that the relations between people are not meaningful or organic but are merely instrumental. One additional feature of people-as-atoms is that the mass is relatively undifferentiated and there is little scope for the pursuit of individual talents. The explanation of these features is simply that they are all characteristics of capitalism, and the remedy lies in some alteration or fundamental reorganization of capitalist society, perhaps through the medium of social planning towards the restoration of conservative virtues.[29] Needless to say, in any concrete study of conservatism one would have to be more specific and exhaustive about the content of conservative thought. Further, no particular conservatism is going to conform perfectly to a constructed ideal-type. In addition there are several reasons for being wary about using the *content* of a system of belief as one's only starting point. Thus, to recognize a methodological point made earlier in this chapter, conservatives and conservatism are involved in a struggle with other social forces and the form of this struggle will partly determine what is said and believed. For example, a conservatism of the early nineteenth century like that of Burke reacts against *competitive* capitalism and measures capitalist society against the image of pre-capitalist society. For conservatives of the twentieth century like Oakeshott, the situation is not so clear, at least partly because of the way that capitalism has changed through intervention by the State—an intervention that conservatives often welcome as mitigating the anarchy of the market.[30] Again, a corollary of struggle is alliance. For example, both socialism and conservatism are formed through their common antipathy to capitalism, despite their very different images of the good society. Thus 'socialist' and 'conservative' theoreticians will often write in remarkably similar terms.[31]

Bearing these qualifications in mind, I want to return to Mannheim's analysis of early nineteenth-century conservative thought in Germany, discussed in the last chapter.[32] For Mannheim, it will be remembered, conservatism, particularly in the rather theoretical form that it took in Germany, was shaped, not only by its opposition to bourgeois society, but also to 'bourgeois' thought, in particular, rationalism. Mannheim's explanation of conservatism is quite conventional. Just as rationalism 'belongs' to a *class* so also does conservatism belong to an alliance of classes through the medium of an intellectual stratum. The difficulty, however, is in understanding why the aristocracy and the petit-bourgeoisie took up the particular *form* of belief that they did. With the rising capitalist class one may say that they adopted rationalism (or individualism for that matter) because these doctrines were appropriate to their economic and political interests. That is, it is the concept of interest that explains why these particular beliefs rather than any others were adopted. For conservatism, however, an interest-explanation is less secure. Thus, it is unclear why the aristocracy's particular economic interests should produce *conservative* doctrines rather than any other. One might perhaps argue that in the early nineteenth century conservatism represented a desperate survival from what Mannheim calls 'feudal-romanticism'. However this merely displaces the problem, for we still need to ask how conservative thought represented the economic and political interests of a dominant feudal class. Again, the problem is why should conservatism be particularly appropriate. It is also a little implausible to use the notion of survival to explain the continuing popularity of conservative ideas into the twentieth century.

Some Difficulties in the Conventional Position

In Part I of this book I have been describing the conventional approach to the sociology of knowledge. Mannheim is a representative figure in this approach (even if he adopts a particular version of it) and can be credited with being the founder of the discipline itself. However, like most other writers in the subject, he constructs his arguments in relation to Marx. Even to the extent that he disagrees with Marx, this is still his point of departure. Nonetheless, as I have tried to indicate in the preceding two chapters, the interpretation of Marx employed by Mannheim is of a particular kind, amounting often to the simple employment of the concepts of class and class-struggle.

Recently, objections have been made to this view of Marx, both as an interpretation of his writings and, more importantly, as a basis for further work. These objections, although perhaps originally technical to Marxism itself, have very obvious implications for the sociology of knowledge. In Part II I shall be considering these objections, while in Part III I shall consider a critique of conventional sociology of knowledge from another point of view entirely, that of phenomenological sociology. Before discussing the details of the Marxist and phenomenological critiques of the conventional position, I indicate just which principal aspects of that position Marxists and phenomenologists criticize.

The Critique from Marxism

(1) Whatever its claims, the conventional position operates with both an oversimplified and a restrictive conception of belief. Firstly, the beliefs that are considered tend to be those of intellectuals and the sources consulted tend to be written texts. The vitally important beliefs of non-intellectuals are not considered.[33] It seems almost to be assumed that intellectuals are effective spokesmen for various interests and that their views are widely shared. Secondly, there is a concentration on formed and articulated specific belief or opinion. This leaves unexamined the much vaguer but probably more important ways of thinking such

as habits of thought, background assumptions, even the structure of language itself. That the social structure might form these fundamental constituents of human thought is more significant than the demonstration that the political theory of individualism can be related to the interests of a capitalist class. This tendency on the part of the conventional approach is represented in the title of the discipline itself—the sociology of *knowledge* or *belief* and may give grounds for preferring a more general designation such as ideology. Thirdly, there is a temptation when talking of ideas or beliefs to think of them as free-floating mental constructs without any anchorage in sets of material practices. By contrast, it should be clear that, for example, it is difficult to talk of someone's religious beliefs without also considering their involvement in religious ritual.

(2) I argued in the last chapter that the conventional position saw beliefs as distorted by the social structure. It has not been made clear exactly in what way they are distorted. We need to have a more precise notion of the ideological *experience*, of the manner in which distorted beliefs appear real and accurate to the believers.

(3) Central to the discussion in this part of the book is the argument that sociological explanation of belief consists in attributing systems of belief to social classes (or, more generally, social groups) via the mechanism of class-interests. I have tried to show in this chapter that the concept of interest is not a particularly powerful explanatory device, although *some* causal mechanism must be specified. This weakness, plus a feeling that analysis in terms of class is not fundamental enough, indicates a closer analysis of the concept of mode of production, which is said to be an underlying social relation explaining the class structure. Such an analysis is also needed to make the relationship between base and superstructure more precise. The view of this relationship described in the Introduction tends to make it a rather vague relation of interaction between belief (or ideology) and economy.

(4) The conventional theory has a rather crude version of what I have called the dominant ideology thesis. In this thesis it is proposed that the dominant class, having command over the means of mental production, is able to impose its system of belief on subordinate classes. In the Introduction I argued that this thesis made a number of incorrect assumptions about the ideological

incorporation of subordinate classes. In addition it can be argued against it that it is not sufficiently precise about the nature of the dominant ideology, it does not conceptualize the means of distribution of belief (including 'class-spokesmen') adequately, and, finally, that it does not have a complete view of the function of ideology in the relationship between society and the human subject.

The Critique from Phenomenology

(1) Phenomenologist sociologists of knowledge, particularly Schütz and Berger and Luckmann, hold that conventional sociology of knowledge is too intellectualized, treating only of theoretical knowledge. This is not quite the same claim as that made by Marxist critics, for the phenomenologists consider that what is neglected is not simply the beliefs of non-intellectuals, but rather the common-sense everyday knowledge that everyone requires in order to live in society. What interests Schütz and Berger and Luckmann therefore is the social construction of *routine* knowledge that is otherwise entirely taken for granted, like the knowledge of how to post a letter or of how to sustain a conversation.

(2) The conventional sociology of knowledge can very easily fall into a mode of expression in which the social structure is seen as 'giving' individual humans their knowledge and beliefs. Phenomenologists, especially Berger and Luckmann, want to restore the autonomy of the human subject in the construction of a system of belief and to get away from the notion of a determining social structure.

(3) At the beginning of this chapter I identified one of the constituents of the conventional sociology of knowledge as being the assumption that the sociologist can describe *systems* of belief. As Mannheim quite clearly realized, there are immense methodological problems even in this first step. Firstly, it is not clear what relation is supposed to hold between beliefs in a system. It plainly will not always be a logical relation for that would be too restrictive. Less confining types of relation like 'affinity' tend to be vague and arbitrary. Further, at first sight at least, the choice of

particular items to make up a system of beliefs also appears arbitrary, depending, as it does, on the theoretical whim of the investigator. This difficulty is compounded by the notion that systems of belief are shared, yet not necessarily held by identifiable individuals. The problem for some writers is therefore: in what sense can these constructions be said to exist?[34]

II
The Critique from Marxism

4 THE NATURE OF IDEOLOGY

The next three chapters deal with some aspects of the recent
Marxist theory of ideology that bear on the sociology of
knowledge. To some extent this is a contrived debate since the two
approaches are rarely brought into direct contact with each other in
the literature. Sociologists and Marxists operate with different
analytical principles, and even different epistemologies and ontologies. However I do not hold that these differences rule out the
possibility of debate; sociologists and Marxists do talk about the
same issue, namely the relationship between consciousness and
social relations.

The Varieties of Belief

Sociologists interested in the social explanation of belief can resort
to a number of sources of evidence. Two are particularly important. For any historical study, written texts are used, as when
Mannheim, in his work on conservative thought, relies exclusively
on the writings of German intellectuals. However it is also possible,
in a contemporary study, to rely on the questionnaire or interview
in which the beliefs of respondents are elicited by the simple device
of asking for them. Both these methods have a tendency to produce
belief as a relatively well-articulated, formed, or theoretical
construction. This evades consideration of other areas of the
relation between thought and society of equal or greater importance. In studying these other areas, ranging from 'common-

sense' to the formation of language itself, there are obvious methodological problems. At least written material and structured interviews seem relatively precise instruments, while the study of the categories of language, for example, is a much vaguer enterprise.

Everybody has views of some kind about the world they live in. As Gramsci says:

> It is essential to destroy the widespread prejudice that philosophy is a strange and difficult thing just because it is the specific intellectual activity of a particular category of specialists or of professional and systematic, philosophers. It must first be shown that all men are 'philosophers', by defining the limits and characteristics of the 'spontaneous philosophy' which is proper to everybody. This philosophy is contained in: 1. language itself, which is a totality of determined notions and concepts and not just of words grammatically devoid of content; 2. 'Common sense' and 'good sense'; 3. popular religion and, therefore, also in the entire system of beliefs, superstitions, opinions, ways of seeing things and of acting, which are collectively bundled together under the name of 'folklore'.[1]

In this passage, Gramsci not only indicates the analytical importance of various levels of thought, namely language, folklore and common-sense, he also treats 'popular thought' in the context of its contrast with the more theoretical doctrines of intellectuals. For him it was the relationship between common-sense and intellectual construction that was crucial, for that relationship is tied to the way that working-class consciousness (common-sense) can become articulated and revolutionary or, alternatively, can become incorporated in a dominant culture.

In the sense that common-sense is the thought of the 'mass' (in Gramsci's term), it is formed by practical experience. It is therefore down to earth and is not distracted by 'fancy quibbles' and 'pseudo-scientific mumbo-jumbo'. In addition, it is experimental and critical. Despite these virtues, common-sense has a number of defects. In particular it is disjointed. 'Its most fundamental characteristic is that it is a conception which, even in the brain of one individual, is fragmentary, incoherent, and inconsequential, in conformity with the social and cultural position of the masses whose philosophy it is.'[2] Perhaps because of this characteristic, common-sense is not self-critical, it is just absorbed routinely as a conception of the world appropriate to a particular social position. Crucially then, this way of thought is engendered in practical activity but cannot go beyond it, for it has 'no clear theoretical consciousness of . . . practical activity'. Indeed, any theoretical understanding that there is may actually be at variance with practical activity. 'One might almost say that he [man-in-the-mass] has two theoretical consciousnesses (or one contradictory consciousness): one which is implicit in his activity and which in reality unites him with all his fellow workers in the practical transformation of the real world; and one, superficially explicit or verbal, which he has inherited from the past and uncritically absorbed.'[3] The existence of this 'dual consciousness' indicates the importance of the relationship of common-sense to intellectual construction, a relationship which can take two forms. Either there can be an imposition of a set of categories, derived from a dominant culture, on the masses in such a way as to perpetuate a dual consciousness, or the intellectual stratum can order and form the mass consciousness as common-sense so as to make it a revolutionary force. This second role is of particular importance for Gramsci in its practical political implications, for he wanted to advocate a particular relationship between the revolutionary party and the working class; to be effective, party intellectuals must be 'organically' related to the working class.

Gramsci's notion that there may be an inconsistency between the life experiences of the working class and their common-sense understandings which derive in part from a dominant culture, also provides a way of interpreting contemporary survey research into working-class beliefs. As I indicated earlier, it may be the case that this research to some extent conceals the components of common-sense. Thus Parkin argues that 'members of the subordinate class are constrained to accept the dominant moral framework as an abstract and perhaps somewhat idealized version of reality, although their life conditions tend to weaken its binding force in the actual conduct of affairs'.[4] From this tension a 'subordinate value system' emerges. This value system (or 'common-sense') will provide a moral frame of reference for the concrete experiences of life, while the dominant value system provides answers for more abstract moral questions. Sociological inquiry, inasmuch as it is couched in abstract terms, may call out a set of responses formed by the dominant ideology and may therefore miss the importance of common-sense. For example, respondents may well express quite negative attitudes towards strikes in general while having favourable attitudes towards strikes in which they participate.[5]

The category of common-sense in Gramsci still refers to a *relatively* precise set of formulations. At a different level is what he refers to as folklore. Hoggart's book *The Uses of Literacy*[6] documents the way in which an oral tradition reflects the life experience and aspirations of the British working class. The complex network of sayings, proverbs, metaphors, superstitions and myths constitutes a socially determined framework that is 'leaned upon as a fixed and still largely trustworthy reference in a world now difficult to understand'.[7] Similarly, the kind of *imagery* that people employ is not randomly chosen but instead clearly reflects the stock of social experience. Doubtless this is plainest in the analysis of literature, but it is also evident in everyday speech as when, for example, someone might refer to a particular action as 'profitable'. Perhaps most fundamental, however, is the way in which language itself is not socially neutral. The central concepts and categories of language are shaped by society. This effective determination of the *manner* in which we think is not, of course, readily apparent. Barthes's work on myths illustrates the pervasive but fundamental influences on ways of thought.[8] He conceives of language in a very broad way, not only as speech or writing, but also as visual images, photography, pictures, or even cinema. The basis for counting all these phenomena as language is that they are all messages with coded structures. Language, conceived in this way, is very open; intrinsically it is not very precise. The result is that a message is *potentially* open to a wide number of interpretations. However messages are *not* typically interpreted widely, for people are given a conceptual structure which permits only a limited number of interpretations. To pursue the image from cryptography, if the language message contains a code, it will be decoded in a fairly restrictive way according to a code-book which is effectively socially derived. Barthes gives an example:

I am at the barber's, and a copy of Paris-Match is offered to me. On the cover, a young Negro in a French uniform is saluting with his eyes uplifted, probably fixed on a fold of the tricolour. All this is the meaning of the picture. But, whether naively or not, I see very well what it signifies to me: that France is a great Empire, that all her sons, without any colour discrimination, faithfully serve under her flag, and that there is no better answer to the detractors of an alleged colonialism than the zeal shown by this Negro in serving his so-called oppressors.[9]

Beliefs and Practices

One of the central claims of the conventional sociology of knowledge is that knowledge, beliefs and ideas cannot be seen as inhabiting an autonomous mental realm but are instead produced and anchored in society. There is still a temptation, however, to see *ideas* as free-floating mental constructs existing in people's heads, even if produced from outside. In the last section I tried to counter the notion that the object of the sociology of knowledge was belief considered as a set of constructed *propositions*. In this section I consider the arguments of Althusser that that object should not be seen as exactly mental, but should instead be seen as a *practice*.[10] Althusser means two things by this proposal. Firstly, ideas (ideologies) should be seen as necessarily linked to their method of production. In particular, there are institutional apparatuses, like the Church or the school system, which 'produce' ideologies. Therefore, ideology cannot be free floating; it always exists in an apparatus. Conversely, the apparatuses are themselves the realization of ideologies. Secondly, and, probably more importantly, ideologies cannot be conceived simply as ideas about the world, but must be seen rather as a kind of 'lived relationship' with the world. At the minimum, ideologies involve not merely thinking about the world but also acting within it. For example, an individual may have 'beliefs' about God, Duty or Justice. However he will also, necessarily, engage in certain actions. If he believes in God, he will go to church and perform the required rituals. 'If he believes in Justice, he will submit unconditionally to the rules of the law, and may even protest when they are violated, sign petitions,

take part in a demonstration, etc.'[11] All these actions are part of the
process by which the ideological apparatus produces ideology. In
sum, ideology exists only in an ideological apparatus which has to
be conceived as producing ideology as a set of beliefs and practices.[12] It might well be argued against Althusser that he has again
restricted the use of the term ideology by tying it too closely to an
apparatus, even if he has thereby moved away from a conception of
ideology as ideas. However he has also appeared to have come a
long way from the notion of ideology as distorted or false belief as
indicated in the term 'false consciousness' used in Part 1(1), for he
occasionally talks of ideology as 'objective'. What could be meant
by this description?

Appearance and Reality

Althusser is partly responsible for a well-marked trend in contemporary Marxist discussions of ideology to replace a conception
of ideologies as simply false representations of reality, to one in
which they do in some way reflect reality. Indeed, it is argued that
the fact that ideologies correspond to everyday experience is the
explanation of their great power over men's minds; belief that is
purely false cannot be so commanding.

Marx frequently seemed to believe that the social world that man
inhabits is shrouded in a kind of conceptual mist.[13] He thought that
in all hitherto existing societies and, in particular, in capitalist
societies, men *systematically* misconceived their world so that their
beliefs, in a very general way, were not exhaustively descriptive of
the 'real' state of affairs. It is very difficult to convey this notion
and Marx frequently relied on metaphor, usually of perceptual
disturbance or malfunction. Unfortunately the metaphors are of
very different kinds with very varied theoretical implications. Thus
men are said to see representations which are not veridical,
illusions, phantoms, phenomena, reflexes, echoes, mists, sub-
limates and inversions in a camera obscura. In their various ways
these metaphors are misleading. 'Mist' and its synonyms are
not right, for they suggest that we may be aware that our beliefs
about the world may be incorrect because of some indistinctness of
intellectual vision. Further, mists dissipate in the morning and

Marx did not believe that the truth was that easily discovered. For him, men did not think that they lived in a misty world. Quite the contrary, the world *seems* clear and sunny, but what we see there is not what is really there. The perceptual difficulty is much more structural; it is not simply a matter of removing a temporary obstacle. 'Illusion' is similarly misleading, for it is not that the perceptual mistake is straightforwardly false. 'Inversion' is too specific, for not all appearances are inversions or mirror images. Besides, as Mepham[14] points out, the camera obscura, in inverting the image, preserves the relations between the elements of the real object, and Marx wants to argue that ideological forms are not necessarily that simple.

All these images of perception are similarly misleading, for they suggest that the source of distortion lies in the perceiving subject or some illusion-creating veil that comes between him and the object perceived. Quite the contrary, there is nothing wrong with the organs of intellectual perception, for it is the reality that deceives. As Godelier says: 'It is not the subject that deceives himself, but reality which deceives him.'[15] Such a remark seems very confusing and its paradoxical quality comes from attempting to suggest that ideologies are simultaneously real and deceptive. If a metaphor has to be used, the best is probably that of concealment. Ideologies do represent and account for social experiences, yet in doing so they also conceal some fundamental features of the world. Some writers prefer to talk, not simply of ideology and reality, but of 'levels of reality' and it is a conception like this that lies behind Althusser's view of ideology as a 'lived relation' to the world. In living in a capitalist society men's relations are essentially ideological for that is how capitalist society presents itself in everyday experience.

The distinction between ideology and 'reality', or between levels of reality, is presented in Marx's *Capital* as a distinction between appearance and reality or between phenomenal forms and real relations.[16] Furthermore, these distinctions almost always arise when Marx is discussing the relationship between the sphere of production and the sphere of circulation.[17] The former is that realm of economic life where value is created, while in the latter, in capitalism, there is the whole series of market exchanges whereby the value created in production is realized and capital is circulated before being put back into the process of production. For Marx, then, additional value is not created in the sphere of circulation, and this is the sense in which the sphere of production is primary and the sphere of circulation is dependent on it. For the creation of value is the fundamental process. The sphere of circulation thus represents a series of economic relationships—the buying and selling of labour-power, and other commodities, the accumulation of capital—which are 'appearances' or 'phenomenal forms' because they are underpinned by a set of 'real relations' whereby value is really created. Nonetheless they are real in the sense that it is in exchange relations that people live their economic lives. For most people, market relations are all important for it is these relations that determine wages and the prices of goods. As Hall says, the sphere of circulation is 'where our spontaneous and everyday common sense perceptions and experiences of the system arise'.[18] These experiences are also real in that, although the process of production is primary, capitalism cannot work without the sphere of circulation, for it is necessary that the value locked up in the commodities produced be realized so that capital can be put to work again.

In sum, capitalism *is* a set of necessary exchange relations in which people participate in their everyday lives. As Marx says: '. . . it is just as natural for the actual agents of production to feel completely at home in these estranged and irrational forms of capital-interest, land-rent, labour-wages, since these are precisely the forms of illusion in which they move about and find their daily occupation.'[19] While 'natural', exchange relations do conceal the more fundamental relations of production. Thus Marx contrasts 'this noisy sphere, where everything takes place on the surface and in view of all men' with 'the hidden abode of production'.[20] Since the everyday reality of capitalism consists in exchange relations, it is not surprising that men will perceive it as such, and further, not surprising that theories of all kinds—political, economic and religious—will be constructed on that basis; the 'phenomenal form, which makes the actual relation invisible, and, indeed, shows the direct opposite of that relation, forms the basis of all the juridical notions of both labourer and capitalist, of all the mystifications of the capitalistic mode of production, of all its illusions as to liberty, of all the apologetic shifts of the vulgar economists'.[21]

These points are aptly illustrated by Marx's treatment of the wage-form. This treatment depends in turn on the theory of the creation of value. In the labourer's working day, part is devoted to creating value equivalent to the labourer's needs for subsistence ('necessary labour time'), while the remainder accrues to the capitalist as surplus value. The capitalist is therefore buying labour-power, the capacity of the worker to work for a certain period of time. In Marx's view, the wage paid is equivalent only to the necessary labour time and therefore the remainder of the working day which creates surplus value is essentially unpaid labour. The 'real relations' in the sphere of production are thus essentially exploitative and the capitalist appropriates surplus value produced by the labourer. However the everyday experience of work is lived in terms defined within the sphere of circulation, for *wages* are determined in a labour market and appear simply as the price of labour. In this market, labour and wages are exchanged as equivalents in the same way as any other act of buying and selling of commodities, giving rise to the notion of a fair wage conceived as a fair *price* for labour. Thus, the whole conception of a wage, which is a real form corresponding to the experience of work, conceals the real relations in which the capitalist extracts a quantity of labour which is not paid for in the wage.

However it is not only a question of concealment of the real by the phenomenal relations. The real relations are also fundamental in the sense that it is they that generate—and explain—the real relations. So a double relationship is involved; phenomenal relations both conceal, and are produced by, real relations. Marx is at pains throughout *Capital* to stress that other theorists have dealt only with the surface appearance while it is the work of science to penetrate to the reality underneath. As he says: 'Vulgar economy . . . everywhere sticks to appearance in opposition to the law which regulates and explains them.'[22] Such a conception of scientificity seems to offer a contrast between science and ideology which parallels that between appearance and reality.

A conception of ideology worked out in terms of the distinction between real and phenomenal forms has evident advantages in that it offers a much more subtle approach to the manner in which ideologies are distorting. We no longer have to hold that people have beliefs which are clearly false and against their class-interests. However, as an account of what ideology is like, it has drawbacks.

Firstly, there must be room for beliefs which are illusory or at least not 'real' in the same sense as phenomenal forms are. Secondly, the distinction is better at making sense of some beliefs than others. For example, theories of the wage-form, or beliefs about individualism, may be seen as descriptive of real relations, yet concealing because of the relationship of the spheres of production and circulation. This is, however, less obviously true of ideas of nationalism, or of religious beliefs.

Commodity Fetishism

Discussion of the distinction between real and phenomenal forms is often bound up with another notion, that of commodity fetishism.[23] Actually, it is not at all clear what the relationship between the two doctrines is and the question that I shall seek to answer is whether the theory of commodity fetishism can give us a *theory* of ideology.

Certainly extravagant claims have been made. Lukacs, for example, said that Marx's chapter on commodity fetishism contained the whole of historical materialism. Such enthusiasm is a little odd, for it rests on a comparatively narrow textual base. Marx used the word 'fetish' throughout *Capital* and there are pre-echoes of the concept, or something like it, in his earlier work, particularly in the *Economic and Philosophical Manuscripts* and *The German Ideology*. The only systematic discussion, however, occurs in Chapter 1, section 4 of *Capital*.[24]

The conventional interpretation of this text is that commodity fetishism represents a process by which men conceive of their social relations as if they were natural things; social relations are *reified*. The argument depends on the notion of a commodity. A man can produce, by his own labour, certain objects for his own use, iron tools, for example; these have a use-value for him. The tools are defined as commodities, however, when they are produced for *exchange*, for use by other people, when they have an 'exchange value'. There is, however, something mysterious about a commodity, a mystery which arises out of the *social* character of the process of the exchange:

The form of wood, for instance, is altered by making a table out of it. Yet for all that, the table continues to be that common, every-day thing wood. But, so soon as it steps forth as a commodity, it is changed into something transcendent . . . it stands on its head, and evolves out of its wooden brain grotesque ideas, far more wonderful than 'table-turning' ever was.[25]

As soon as commodities are being produced for exchange, the labour-power involved assumes a social character. But since the producers do not come into social contact with each other until they actually exchange their products, the social character of each producer's labour does not show itself *except* in the act of exchange.

In other words, the labour of the individual asserts itself as a part of the labour of society only by means of the relations which the act of exchange establishes directly between the products, and indirectly, through them, between the producers.[26]

Therefore:

. . . the social character of men's labour appears to them as an objective character stamped upon the product of that labour; because the relation of the producers to the sum total of their own labour is presented to them as a social relation, existing not between themselves, but between the products of their labour . . . There it's on a definite social relation between men, that assumes, in their eyes, the fantastic form of a relation between things.[27]

Men's thinking about the social relations involved in their work is characterized by a fetishism whereby beliefs about the physical products of labour, and their exchange, substitute for, and masks, the social relations themselves; in a very general way, men characterize their social relations as relations between things; social relations are *reified*. Further, it is not just that social relations are reified in this way, for there is also a sense in which men are *dominated* by their characterization of their social relations as reified.

Men therefore see their activities as being ruled by objects which are natural, taken-for-granted features of the world, rather than by social relations which they have a hand in making and, perhaps, also in unmaking. As Marx says: 'Their own social action takes the form of the action of objects, which rule the producers instead of being ruled by them.'[28]

Since the tendency to fetishistic thinking arises only when objects are produced by men, not for their own consumption but for exchange, the more a society is dominated by commodity production (that is, production for exchange) the more it will be dominated by fetishistic thinking.[29] Thus, Marx contrasts feudal societies with capitalist ones. In capitalist societies, goods are produced with the quite conscious intention of exchange for money; such societies will be dominated by fetishistic thinking. But in feudal societies, inasmuch as they are based on relations of personal dependence (not wage-labour) and in which transactions take the form of services and payments in kind, 'There is no necessity for labour and its products to assume a fantastic form different from their reality.'[30] So fetishistic thinking is not *specific* to the capitalist mode of production, but that mode encourages it more than any other one that has historically existed.

Marx's account of commodity fetishism has been made the basis of several theories of ideology. Lukacs, for example, in his early work *History and Class Consciousness*,[31] is largely responsible for the introduction of the concept of reification and for interpreting Marx's views in *Capital* as providing theoretical support for that concept. For Lukacs, the process by which the production of goods became the production of commodities for exchange, was more or less equivalent to a process of reification, the basis of which 'is that a relation between people takes on the character of a thing and thus acquires a "phantom objectivity", an autonomy that seems so strictly rational and all-embracing as to conceal every trace of its fundamental nature, the relation between people.'[32] The most important effect of the process of reification is the *rationalization* of men's everyday conduct, a rationalization so pervasive and complete that it literally affects every aspect of life. In particular, men's work lives are made rationalized and calculable, leading to a 'progressive elimination of the qualitative, human, and individual attributes of the worker'. An increasing division of labour means that the worker loses contact with his product; rationalization means specialization. The rationalization goes further in infecting the discharge of bureaucratic tasks, the conduct of the business of the State, and ultimately, the whole structure of human thought, particularly of modern science. In an important way, Lukacs's argument about rationalization has affinities with what is often seen as conservative thinking.[33] For both, what rationalization and specialization have destroyed is the essential *totality* of human experience, its organic unity, which is essential to a full and humanized life. As Lukacs says: 'The specialization of skills leads to the destruction of every image of the whole.'[34] Indeed, this concern with the importance of organic unity, actually central to much of the argument in *History and Class Consciousness*, appears almost grafted on to Marx's notions of commodity fetishism, for Lukacs does not successfully establish the *theoretical* connections between reification and rationalization. There is one last point concerning Lukacs's account of commodity fetishism as reification. In the interpretation of Marx's views on the subject, I suggested that commodity fetishism is not specific to the capitalist mode of production, but is encouraged by it more than any other mode. For Lukacs, however, fetishism is a 'specific problem of our age', since there is a qualitative difference between societies in which the commodity form is dominant, 'permeating every expression of life', and those in which it makes merely an episodic appearance. In the first case, in capitalist societies, the commodity form has effectively taken over, while in the second it is scarcely noticeable.

Berger and Pullberg[35] also use the concept of reification in their analysis of consciousness, although their account has effectively moved away from any basis in commodity fetishism. For them, as for Lukacs, reification is a process whereby the social world is conceived entirely as a set of objective things which are divorced from man's control and have power over him; it is a 'thing-like facticity separated from its human source'. Thus social structure in general is perceived by the individual to be external and coercive. People, for example, perceive their behaviour in roles as something in which they have no choice. 'Roles are reified by detaching them from human intentionality and expressivity, and transforming them into an inevitable destiny for their bearers.'[36] Although reification is not a necessary and intrinsic quality of human social life, it is present, as a matter of fact, in most societies. In this, Berger and Pullberg are in clear disagreement with both Marx and Lukacs, who insist that reification is almost entirely confined to capitalist societies. The reason for the disagreement lies in Berger and Pullberg's rejection of the nature of the commodity being the basis for reification. They instead 'suspect' that the explanation lies in something that is almost a constant of human nature— and hence present in many different kinds of society—namely the 'fundamental terrors of human existence'. However, one respect in which all three authors do agree is that reification is a process that affects all spheres of thought, including that of science. For example, for Berger and Pullberg, a sociology that spoke of roles determining what people do, is a reified science.

It is common to find reification spoken of as if a reified consciousness was one prey to *illusions*; social relations are not really things, so to think so is to be merely deluded. Berger and Pullberg come very close to saying this, while it is unclear what Lukacs thinks.[37] With Marx, however, it is more straightforward. In much the same way as he argues that phenomenal forms are not illusions but are realities which conceal, reifications do represent the reality of capitalist social relations. Thus it should be clear that capitalism *is* the exchange of commodities, of things; the social relations between producers *do* consist of exchanges, and that is the only way in which the labour of the individual can be part of the labour of society. In a passage which the notion of reification as illusion can treat only as an aberration, Marx suggests that to the producers 'the relations connecting the labour of one individual with that of the rest appear, not as direct social relations betwen individuals at work, *but as what they really are*, material relations between persons and social relations between things'.[38] Reification is not illusion; it is a reality that conceals; the 'exchange of products' conceals 'the social character of the labour'. The same points apply to Marx's critique of the economists of his day. In a sense they are correct in their analyses, for they are accurately describing the content of a capitalist economy. At another level, however, they are mistaken, in that they take capitalism out of its historical context and make the social relations of capitalism *natural* phenomena.

All these rather different accounts of reification tend to use the concept as if it had a unitary character. However it is clear that it is not one concept, but three. There is firstly the process by which social relations are made into things. For example, in capitalism, it may be that people express their social relations by an exchange of things or gifts in such a way that the exchange of gifts *becomes* the relationship. Secondly, the social world appears natural and permanent rather than socially constructed. For example, it is often said that it is in the nature of women to care for children but it is not natural to men. Thirdly, the social world appears as dominating and outside human control. For example, the necessity of going to work in the morning appears coercive. Now these three concepts together do make for a neat theory; the *social* relations of capitalism, for example, are made thing-like, appear as permanent and natural features of the social world, and then seem to dominate men's activities. However they are not *logically* related; for example to speak of a woman's role as natural is not necessarily to speak of it as thing-like. The difficulty that this point creates is that not all the three elements of reification may be equally explained by the theory of commodities outlined earlier.

So far, I have argued that the conventional view of Marx's account of commodity fetishism in *Capital* is that provided by Lukacs; that is, commodity fetishism is really about reification. As an interpretation of the text, let alone as a theory in its own right, this view seems to me to be gravely deficient. A clue lies in Marx's use of the word 'fetishism' which seems to have been borrowed from his anthropological reading. In this usage it refers to the manner in which an object, animate or inanimate, is included in religious ritual. The object, or fetish, is worshipped or is accorded miraculous powers which make it sacred. In some ways this process of fetishism is the reverse of the process of reification. It is not the rendering of social relations as things, but the rendering of things as entities possessing powers. In many places, Marx's work seems to follow this latter usage, often, yet again, in the form of a metaphor. Thus, he compares social relations between men to the 'mist enveloped regions of the religious world. In that world the productions of the human brain appear as independent beings *endowed with life*. . ... So it is in the world of commodities with the products of men's hands. This I call the fetishism which attaches itself to the products of labour, so soon as they are produced as commodities . . . .'[39]

In fact, Marx is not describing one process under the label of fetishism but two. The first is reification. The second is a process that I shall call *mystification* in which, as I have said above, men grant objects powers to do things of their own nature, when in fact these powers derive from social relations. It is important to realize how different these two processes are. The first is, as we have seen, a relation of concealment rather than illusion. With mystification, however, it is more likely that the powers given to things are illusory. So Marx speaks of the 'illusions of the monetary system' or of 'natural objects with strange social properties'. He points to the way that money capital is treated, not as a social relation, but as a thing which is capable of expanding itself, of generating money-interest.

Indeed it is possible that Marx muddled the two processes up in that he moves from one process to another in the same passage without notice. However the problem is not primarily one of identifying different processes. There is also a theoretical problem. We do at least have a *theory* of reification, which is explained in terms of the nature of the commodity. It is not a complete theory for it appears to depend initially on a limiting assumption of independent producers exchanging commodities. It is not absolutely clear how it would apply to workers who are not exchanging commodities with each other, but are instead selling their labour-power to a capitalist. It might be argued that everyone is involved in work processes in which commodities are produced for exchange, and that this results in a reified consciousness somehow being generally diffused throughout society. However, not only do we not know how this diffusion takes place, it is also plain that being directly involved in the exchange of commodities is rather different from being indirectly involved via the sale of labour-power.

Nonetheless, so far I am arguing only that the theory of reification is incomplete. Either it is in need of further theoretical elements, or it is limited in its scope in that it applies most particularly to the social relations of production of capitalism very strictly conceived. But Marx does not appear to provide a theory of mystification at all. That is he does not tell us how it is that men confer powers on things. Unlike reification, which primarily demands an analysis of the mechanisms of capitalism because that system *is* an exchange of things, mystification seems to require an analysis of mental processes, because the problem is to explain why it is that men have certain beliefs about the world (and this may be related to the manner in which mystification is rather more a process of illusion).

It might plausibly be argued that reification and mystification are not two separate processes but two aspects of the same process or perhaps one process—mystification—laid on top of the other and necessarily following on from it. Thus men may see their social relations as thing-like and natural and they may then ascribe powers to those things. For example, we have seen how, when goods are produced for exchange, the exchange of physical objects is the only relationship between the producers, and consequently men come to see only this relationship of things not the social relationship that it conceals. Added to this is the fact that an economy based on the exchange of commodities is ultimately an economy based on money. This makes the process of reification even more pronounced, for it is not only a question of the direct exchange of commodities but rather of that exchange mediated by an abstract thing, money. 'It is, however, just this ultimate money-form of the world of commodities that actually conceals, instead of disclosing, the social character of private labour. . . .'[40] However with money acquiring importance as a medium of exchange, men give it the ability to do things by itself, for example, to generate interest. In other words men mystify money; '. . . gold and silver, when serving as money, did not represent a social relation between producers, but were natural objects with strange social properties.'[41] So, in a case like this (though not invariably in Marx or his commentators) mystification attends on reification. Although this makes better sense of the construction of ideology, it still does not illuminate mystification very much. Doubtless, if money is mystified in this way, the powers that it is given are, so as to speak, 'borrowed' from the social relationship of producers which underlies it; money has the powers which properly belong elsewhere. But how is this borrowing effected?

I turn now to a consideration of the utility of the theory of commodity fetishism for an overall theory of ideology. In part, this involves measuring the theory against conventional sociology of knowledge and the problems which it attempts to tackle. Firstly, reification and mystification (I shall refer to these jointly as fetishism) do not exhaust the forms that ideology takes. It may well be that fetishistic thinking is typical of capitalist society, but one will still need a theory to approach thinking which is not fetishistic. Secondly, fetishism does not tell us a great deal about the *specific* content of belief-systems, only that, in capitalist societies, they will tend to be fetishistic, a rather general characteristic. For example, the idea that beliefs are fetishistic does not help to explain the pervasiveness of individualism in eighteenth-century social, economic and political thought, or why that individualism is different from the concept of individuality often associated with the Romantic movement of the early nineteenth century. Thirdly, there is something of a theoretical gap between the relatively specific claim that commodity fetishism arises out of the production of goods for exchange and the more general assertion that fetishistic thinking is characteristic of society as a whole. To move from one to the other requires some additional theoretical elements which suggest how the original fetishism is amplified or distributed. A comment made by a critic of Lukacs applies to the whole discussion of the subject.

> But it is important to notice that this domination has virtually no institutional apparatus whatever. It is simply 'pure ideology'—the unseen rays of a hidden centre of the universe—commodity fetishism . . . Lukacs' whole account of bourgeois ideological domination is reduced to the invisible emanations of reification from commodities, which radiate out to bleach the consciousness of the inhabitants of capitalist society—what is strikingly and completely missing in Lukacs' account is, of course, the whole institutional superstructure of bourgeois class-power. . . .[42]

To take a naive example, one needs to know how it is that those *not* involved in the production of commodities share in fetishistic thinking. Lastly, there are some difficulties about *who* it is that employs fetishistic categories. The doctrine implies that all men, all groups of men, are imprisoned in phenomenal forms. However one might well want to suggest that not all systems of beliefs are *similarly* fetishistic and some groups or social classes might be better placed than others to penetrate phenomenal forms to the real social relations. Similarly, one of the major problems in the conventional sociology of knowledge is to explain the *differences* in the beliefs characteristic of different social groups, particularly social classes. The theory of commodity fetishism, at best, gives us an account of the general character of beliefs in capitalist society, as in the way in which 'bourgeois' thought differs from 'aristocratic' thought. Similarly, as Marx pointed out, the beliefs of social classes are not uniform over time; the thought characteristic of the rise of a social class to social, political and economic power, will differ from that appropriate to its dominance, or, indeed, its subsequent fall.

The burden of these comments is that the theory of commodity fetishism, even ignoring certain internal weaknesses, is not, by itself, very good at explaining certain traditional problems in the sociology of knowledge. Indeed, the solution would appear to be to marry the theory up with elements drawn from the conventional theory, particularly to cope with the problem of institutional mediation. Lukacs recognizes this, though not quite in these terms. Despite the tendency of his account of reification to imply that all social classes are similarly involved, he wants to say that the bourgeoisie have a more deeply reified consciousness than the proletariat. To do this he has to introduce a new idea: 'The proposition with which we began, viz. that in capitalist society reality is—immediately—the same for both the bourgeoisie and the proletariat remains unaltered. But we may now add that this same reality employs the motor of class-interests to keep the bourgeoisie imprisoned within this immediacy, while forcing the proletariat to go beyond it.'[43] So Lukacs's theory of reification involves a concept crucial to the conventional sociology of knowledge—class-interest.

The theory of commodity fetishism has a number of strengths, not least of which is the subtlety of its approach to the manner in which ideology is distorting. Just as it may lack some of the basic elements of the more conventional account, it also has the advantage that it avoids any implication that ideology is something one class 'does' to another. Instead of a relatively crude image of a class imposing its beliefs on another class to suit its class-interests, the theory of commodity fetishism points to the way in which ideological categories arise out of the structure of the capitalist mode of production itself. I shall return to this point in the next chapter.

Science and Ideology

I have argued earlier in this book that a standard problem in the sociology of knowledge is that of relativism. The argument is that if knowledge is socially determined, then it must be false, and that if all knowledge is so determined, then all knowledge is false and we have no way of deciding between true and false knowledge. A special case of this argument revolves round the notion of interest. Beliefs are formed by class-interest. To the extent that they are so formed, they are false (or partial). Therefore, either there are beliefs that are not formed by class-interest, or all knowledge is false (see Part I). I argued in *Chapter 3* that this kind of argument rested on the false assumption that social determination or class-interest necessarily produced false beliefs. A demonstration of the social origin of a set of beliefs does not necessarily entail its falsity. However, what is of more immediate sociological interest is that such a demonstration might indicate the *probability* of falsity. This admission does make the establishment of the methods by which we arrive at correct knowledge of some importance. If there is a probability that particular kinds of social determination distort certain sets of beliefs (make them ideological), then we have to be clear how we show them to be distortions. Effectively this involves the delimitation of science, or a special science at any rate, a project largely outside the scope of this book. However I do want to touch briefly on one aspect of the problem.

The distinction between phenomenal forms and real relations raises similar difficulties. It has been argued that in capitalist societies, thinking, both common-sense and theoretical, tends to be ideological in the sense that it is fetishistic or expressed in phenomenal forms. The problem, then, is to *recognize* ideology. After all, it is in the very nature of a phenomenal form not to carry its hallmark stamped upon it. How does one know when one has penetrated through phenomenal forms to the real relations underneath? This again returns us to the problem of science, for Marx argues that it is the task of science to reveal real relations. Thus, in contrasting the phenomenal form of 'wages' with the real relation of 'value of labour power', he says 'the former appear directly and spontaneously as current modes of thought, the latter must first be discovered by science. Classical Political Economy nearly touches the true relation of things, without, however, consciously formulating it. This it cannot do so long as it sticks to its bourgeois skin.'[44]

For Marx, therefore, the distinction between phenomenal form and real relations is parallel to that between ideology and science. This is the basis on which Althusser constructs his account of science and of the scientificity of Marxism. Briefly, Althusser argues that the mark of science is its open structure which permits development and refinement of knowledge. Ideology on the other hand is a closed circular system in which the questions asked simply confirm the assumptions of the system; it is like looking in a mirror. However science is not open in the sense that its knowledge is tested against the outside world. There are no *external* guarantees of scientificity lying outside the system of knowledge. There is, in other words, a rigid distinction between theoretical knowledge in sciences, and knowledge of the external world. Science has, therefore, according to Althusser, a 'radical inwardness' in which the security of knowledge is defined by the internal procedures of rigour and systematicity, not by efficacy in dealing with the real world. These differences indicate a difference in the *function* of the two practices, science and ideology. Thus 'ideology, as a system of representations, is distinguished from science in that in it, the practico-social function is more important than the theoretical function . . .'.[45] An alternative way of putting this is to say that ideology is regulated or produced by interests other than the pursuit of knowledge.

Althusser's view of science is like that offered in Part I(2) in that it stresses the methodological differences between science and non-science, even if it may still not offer a great deal of help in recognizing ideology. However the two views are unlike, in that Althusser believes very strongly that science is outside social determination; it is an autonomous practice (the Doctrine of Autonomous Science of Part I(1)). In this he differs sharply from Lukacs whose notion of science is like the Doctrine of Proletarian Science discussed in Part I(1). Althusser holds to the conception of autonomous science because to believe that it is subject to social determination is to deform it, to make it like ideology. Not only is this assumption incorrect, it is also unnecessary for Marxism. Bourgeois science is not *necessarily* false because it is bourgeois.

---

5 THE CONCEPT OF MODE OF PRODUCTION

There is no concept which has a more central place in the recent revival of Marxist theory than that of the mode of production. Elaboration of this concept partly takes the form of a rigorous and systematic investigation of different types of economy, considering their 'laws of motion', the relationship between those who labour with the means of the production and others, the manner in which the surplus product is appropriated, and so on. It also involves a close interest in the way that the economy relates both to the polity and ideology and hence clearly bears on the issues discussed in Part I. Debate surrounding the concept is not, however, confined to these issues which are, after all, hardly new to Marxism, but has broadened out to include a whole range of methodological and philosophical considerations. Thus, there is argument about the causal primacy to be given to the economy, the definition of a Marxist science, and the role of human agents and social classes *vis-à-vis structures* of social *relations*.

To place the concept of mode of production in its proper context, we must return to the doctrine of base and superstructure first discussed in Part I(1). 'Base' is understood to comprise the forces plus the relations of production, while 'superstructure' tends to be simply a residual category including at least the polity, religious and educational institutions, and systems of belief. The actual relationship between base (or 'economy') and superstructure is a matter for debate. Engels, particularly in the period after Marx's death, was anxious to emphasize, as against 'vulgar' Marxists, that the superstructure was not simply determined by the base, but had, on the contrary, a certain autonomy. Engels's conclusion is, then, that the economic is of final and decisive importance, but the superstructure may still influence the base.

As I have indicated before, Marx did not specifically tackle the question of ideology in his later work. However, it is possible to argue that the whole of his major work, *Capital*, is founded on a theory about the relation of superstructure to base, a theory that is at variance with the conventional account described above, in that, at the very least, it emphasizes the autonomy of the superstructure even more.

Marx argues that, in capitalism, of the value produced by the labourer in a working day, a certain part is equal to that which is required for the maintenance of the labourer (or the 'reproduction of his labour-power'). This part is referred to as necessary labour. The remainder is surplus labour and is appropriated by the capitalist. Thus: working day = necessary labour-time + surplus labour-time. Necessary labour can be treated as relatively constant, though it will vary over long periods of time, being determined socially. Therefore, the longer the working day, the greater is the mass of surplus labour extracted by the capitalist (other things being equal, an important condition). The determination of the working day is therefore of crucial importance to capitalist and labourer alike, who clearly have contradictory interests. Marx is quite clear that it is the state that limits the length of the working day: 'these acts [Factory Acts] curb the passion of capital for a limitless draining of labour-power, by forcibly limiting the working-day by state regulations, made by a state that is ruled by capitalist and landlord.'[1] The State acts in this way, despite the political dominance of the capitalist class, because it responds to the struggle between capital and labour (though Marx is certainly not precise as to the relationship between state policies and the class-struggle). Thus he says: 'Hence it is that in the history of capitalist production, the determination of what is a working-day, presents itself as the result of a struggle, a struggle between collective capital i.e. the class of capitalists, and collective labour, i.e. the working-class.'[2] So, in this example, a superstructural element, the State, is not only autonomous of the base, but is actually crucial in the determination of certain elements of the economy. Furthermore, Marx makes clear how state policy is informed by moral beliefs about the harm done by overwork as evidenced in the reports of the English Factory Inspectors.

There are other points in *Capital* where Marx is effectively demonstrating a view of the relationship between base and superstructure. Of perhaps more significance for the analysis of ideology, is his examination of the exchange of commodities. In order for commodities 'to go to market', they must have owners or guardians. For them to be exchanged, 'their guardians must place themselves in relation to one another, as persons whose will resides in those objects, and must behave in such a way that each does not appropriate the commodity of the other, and part with his own, except by means of an act done by mutual consent. They must, therefore, mutually recognize in each other the rights of private proprietors.'[3] In sum, the juridical relation of ownership, definitely superstructural, is necessary for the exchange of commodities, an economic phenomenon.

The significance of these examples is that they show that the relationship between the superstructure and the economic base is not merely one of causal interaction or of relative autonomy. They show instead that the economy will not work unless elements of the superstructure, whether they be polity or ideology, persistently and continuously intervene in the workings of the economy; the superstructure is a *condition of existence* of the base.

The concept of base and superstructure trades necessarily on an architectural image; there is a base on which is built a super-structure. Inherent in the image is the notion, central to Marxism, that the economy is, in some way, primary; it is *basic*. However the idea of condition of existence appears to upset the image. Cohen, however, believes that it is a question of choosing the right image, which can be expressed as follows. 'Consider four struts driven into the ground, each protruding the same distance above it. They are unstable. They wobble at winds of force 3. Now attach a roof to the four struts, which renders them stable at all winds under force 6. Of this roof one can say: (i) it is supported by struts, and (ii) it renders them more stable.'[4] Some notion of the superstructure being a condition of existence of the base, which is itself still in some sense primary, is essential to the concept of the mode of production. I turn now to a more systematic discussion of the concept, starting with the work of Althusser.

The Althusserian Conception of Mode of Production

Althusser believes that he is introducing a new conception of mode of production. This conception cannot be represented in the base/superstructure image which, for him, has, unavoidably, too much of the idea of a determinant base. It conveys the notion of a social totality which is simply the expression of a single element; it is an *expressive totality*. At the same time he wishes to avoid the opposite of the expressive totality, which is a view of society as composed of interacting and more or less equal factors. His solution is a view of the social totality 'whose unity, far from being the expressive or "spiritual" of Leibniz's or Hegel's whole, is constituted by a certain type of complexity, the unity of a structured whole containing what can be called levels or instances which are distinct and "relatively autonomous", and co-exist within this complex structural unity, articulated with one another according to specific determination, fixed in the last instance by the level or instance of the economy.'[5]

Before looking at this definition in more detail, a brief digression into one of Althusser's methodological tenets is necessary. He distinguishes, as do many of those who have followed him, between analysis of the mode of production in the abstract, and analysis of concrete existing societies, which cannot be considered as if they were composed of a single mode of production. An explication of a mode of production must take the form of showing how the economy works, how the relations of production relate to the forces of production, and how the economy relates to other instances or structures. The construction of a mode is a purely 'internal' matter which does not involve any reference to existing societies. There is no question, therefore, of testing the mode of production as a model against reality. This, for Althusser, would be 'empiricism' (see his view of science, discussed in the previous chapter). There are rules as to what would count as a proper mode of production, but these rules are internal to Marxism; modes are properly constructed if they properly combine certain concepts within Marxism, not if they match up well to the evidence provided by an examination of existing societies. A number of modes are proper in this sense. Besides capitalism, the modes of feudalism, slavery and primitive communism can be formulated. In my view there are serious difficulties in the distinction between analysis of the 'pure' mode and analysis of real societies (or social formations) and I shall touch on these later in the chapter. However one useful consequence of the distinction is that it enables us to read Marx's *Capital*, not as a more or less adequate description of capitalist *societies*, but as a depiction of the capitalist mode of production. Of course such an abstract analysis may be *useful* in considering actual capitalist societies and Marx does include discussions of English society throughout *Capital*. These discussions should be seen, however, as illustrations, not tests, of his theory.

In looking at Althusser's work, I consider first his construction of the concept of the mode of production and then the application of such an analysis to the discussion of real societies. From the definition provided at the beginning of this section, it is clear that he sees a mode of production as a complex relation of *structures* one of which is the economy. An exhaustive discussion of contemporary Marxist views of the economy is outside the purposes of this book, but a brief account of Althusser's version is as follows. [6]

The economy consists of three elements, the *labourer*, the *means of production*, which comprises both the materials worked on and the means by which this work is done, and the *non-worker*, who appropriates the product. All modes of production are characterized by these three elements, but what differentiates one mode from another is the manner in which the elements are combined. There are two kinds of relation that can hold between elements, a relation of possession and a relation of property. Possession indicates the relationship between the labourer and the means of production; either he can be in possession of them, controlling and directing them, or not. In the relation of property, the non-labourer is owner, either of the means of production or labour-power, or both, and is thus enabled to appropriate the surplus product. As I have indicated, economies differ from one another, as the relations between the invariant elements differ.

> In the Capitalist mode of production, both connexions [relations] can indeed be characterized by a 'separation': the labourer is 'separated' from all the means of production; he is stripped of all property (save that of his labour-power); but at the same time, as a human individual, the labourer is 'separated'

from any ability to set in motion the instruments of social labour by himself; he has lost his craft skill, which no longer corresponds to the means of labour.[7]

However, in the feudal mode of production, there is a separation in the relation of property, with the non-labourer appropriating the surplus product, but the labourer has possession of the means of production.

Despite the labelling of one of the relations between elements of the economy, the relation of 'property', Althusser is insistent that this is not property in the strictly legal sense; it is an economic relation, referring to the ability of the non-labourer to appropriate the product. There is thus an *analytical* separation of property as an economic relation and property as a legal relation. Nonetheless, and this is crucial to Althusser's conception of a mode of production, a legal system is a condition of existence of the economy: 'the whole of the economic structure of the capitalist mode of production from the immediate process of production to circulation and the distribution of the social product, presupposes the existence of a *legal system*; the basic elements of which are the *law of property and the law of contract*.'[8]

It is not just the legal system that is a condition of existence of the economy. The whole superstructure of political and ideological relations is also required. For Althusser, then, the mode of production consists of a number of structures related together, but also partly independent. There is never a moment when the economy is 'pure'; it is always associated with, and is inconceivable without, the political and ideological structures. At the same time, ideology and politics are not deducible from, and are not expressions of, the economy; they have their own laws of development. This is a theme to which Althusser returns again and again throughout his work. For example, he says: 'this shows that certain relations of production presuppose the existence of a legal–political and ideological superstructure as a condition of their peculiar existence . . . the relations of production cannot therefore be thought in their concept while abstracting from their specific superstructural conditions of existence.'[9] In contrast to the conventional Marxism discussed in Part I(1), Althusser is presenting a view of the relation between economy, on the one hand, and ideology and politics, on the other, which is not a question of the former determining the latter or of simple interaction, but is one in which the economy *must* have superstructural elements. However it is also true that, in stressing the autonomy and indispensability of politics and ideology, Althusser is at risk of disposing of a principle that more or less defines Marxism—the primacy of the economy.

In the definition of the social totality (or mode of production) quoted earlier, Althusser suggests that the totality is a complex relationship of structures, levels, or instances, 'fixed in the last instance by the level or instance of the economy'.

In Althusser's work generally, the primacy of the economy is established by the concept of *determination in the last instance.* In the last instance, the mode of production is determined by the economy. However, this does not mean that in the long run, or given enough time, the economy is determinant, for this might undermine the vital significance that Althusser gives to the superstructure: 'in History, these instances, the superstructures are never seen to step respectfully aside when their work is done or, when the time comes, as his pure phenomena, to scatter before His Majesty The Economy as he strides along the royal road of the Dialectic. From the first moment to the last, the lonely hour of the "last instance" never comes.'[10] So what is the role of the economy?

The economy is *determinant* in that it establishes which structure within a mode of production is to be *dominant.* That is, the economy in some modes of production is such that it requires (as a condition of its existence) that some other element dominate. Thus Marx says that the economy does not dominate in

> the middle ages in which Catholicism, nor for Athens and Rome, where politics, reigned supreme. . . . This much, however, is clear, that the middle ages could not live on Catholicism, nor the ancient world on politics. On the contrary, it is the economic conditions of the time that explain why here politics and there Catholicism played the chief part. It requires but a slight acquaintance with the history of the Roman Republic, for example, to be aware that its secret history is the history of its landed property.[11]

In other modes, especially in capitalism, the economy itself is dominant (though it still requires ideological and political conditions of existence). This conception of 'determination in the last instance' is an extremely ingenious one, and it deserves more extended treatment than it receives in Althusser's writings. For example, one needs to know what precisely is the meaning of dominance, or, rather, what are its indices.

In sum, Althusser's concept of the mode of production is a systematic attempt to establish both the independent significance of the superstructure and the primacy of the economy. This, he believes, was also Marx's project. 'Marx has at least given us the "two ends of the chain", and has told us to find out what goes on between them; on the one hand, determination in the last instance by the economic . . .; on the other, the relative autonomy of the super-structure and their specific effectivity.'[12] En route to his conception, Althusser coins some new terms. The notion that the social whole is composed of a complex set of structures, partly autonomous, partly conditions of existence for each other, leads him to say that each of these structures is *overdetermined*. Any structure 'is inseparable from its formal conditions of existence, and even from the instances it governs; it is radically affected by them, determining, but also determined in one and the same movement . . .'.[13] Nonetheless, the social whole is not just any combination of elements in any order. As we have seen, it has a structure resulting from the fact that one instance is dominant; it has, as Althusser says, a *structure-in-dominance*.

Althusser's theory, and the reading of Marx that supports it, is determined by his opposition to Hegel and Hegelian elements in Marx. Althusser accuses Hegel of reducing 'the infinite diversity of a historically given society' to a single principle which determines everything else. Hegel is thus committing the sin of oversimplicity, when what is needed is the assertion of the overdetermination of all the elements in a mode of production by all the others. Inasmuch as Hegel held that ideal factors determined material ones, Marxists must not, Althusser argues, simply invert Hegel, for that would be to repeat his mistake of having one element, in this case the economy, determining the others in a simple way. The Marxist conception must indicate a new relationship between new terms.

I started this account of Althusser's concept of the mode of production with a distinction between analysis of the mode of production considered in the abstract and analysis of concrete, existing societies (or social formations). A mode of production is never found 'pure', for all societies are mixtures of modes or elements of modes. Actually, 'mixture' is the wrong word, for the crucial point is that the modes of production present in a society *relate* to one another and one of the important clues to the nature of a society is the manner in which modes of production articulate within it. The most significant relations that exist between modes is that of domination and subordination. For example, according to Poulantzas, 'capitalist societies at the start of the 20th century were composed of (i) elements of the feudal mode of production (ii) the form of simple commodity production and manufacture . . . and (iii) the capitalist mode of production in its competitive and monopoly forms.'[14] However, these societies are referred to as capitalist, because the capitalist mode of production dominates the others. The fact that one mode may be subordinate does not mean that it is in the process of disappearing. The articulation of modes in a society is not, in other words, merely a phenomenon of the transition from the dominance of one mode to the dominance of another. It is instead a permanent feature, as modes are not *always* competitive and the presence of a subordinate mode can be functional for the dominant mode.[15] This complex view of societies opens the way for a subtle analysis of ideology, for we no longer have to think of societies as dominated by one ideology. They are instead characterized by ideologies appropriate to the various modes present, dominated by the ideology of the dominant mode. Moreover, these various ideologies are not isolated from one another, they relate to each other in ways determined by the history of each society. Althusser believes that his view, in escaping from a 'vulgar' conventional Marxism, in which the economy is primary, means

(1) that a revolution in the structure does not ipso facto modify the existing superstructures and particularly the ideologies at one blow (as it would if the economic was the sole determining factor), . . . (2) that the new society produced by the Revolution may itself ensure the survival, that is, the reactivation, of older elements through both the forms of its new superstructures and specific (national and international) 'circumstances'.[16]

Mode of Production in the Early Work of Hindess and Hirst

Althusser has been very influential in the rapid growth of Marxist writing on the concept of mode of production. The early writings of Hindess and Hirst[17] show that influence even if they may disagree with many of Althusser's conclusions. From the point of view of the themes of this book, their work is interesting in that it represents a systematic attempt to examine a number of different modes of production, by considering the relationship of the economy to its ideological and political conditions of existence.

Hindess and Hirst have a particularly radical view of the distinction between production of the *concept* of a mode of production, whose 'validity can be determined only within the field of concepts which specify the general definition of mode of production'; and the analysis of concrete societies.[18] The economy, referred to as mode of production, a sense quite different from Althusser's, is defined in the following way:

> A mode of production is an articulated combination of relations and forces of production structured by the dominance of the relations of production. The relations of production define a specific mode of appropriation of surplus-labour and the specific form of social distribution of the means of production corresponding to that mode of appropriation of surplus-labour. For example, capitalist relations of production define a mode of appropriation of surplus-labour which works by means of commodity exchange.[19]

'Forces of production' refers to the combination of three elements; labour, the material which is worked, and the tools and equipment which perform the labour. These elements may be combined in different ways. For example, there may be different forms of co-operation of individual labourers. One may say, then, that there will be different *labour processes* defined by different *relationships* between the elements, not by the elements themselves. The forces of production are then dominated, or organized, by the relations of production, to produce a particular distribution of the product and a particular relation to the means of production.[20]

So far we are given an analysis of the economy (or mode of production) as an abstract theoretical entity that does not actually exist. For a particular mode to exist in a society it must have certain conditions of existence, economic, as well as political and ideological. For example

> it is clear that the capitalist and the slave modes of production require that certain forms of monetary calculation are performed by particular agents of production. The existence of these modes therefore depends on the maintenance of the ideological social relations in which these forms of calculation are developed and individuals are trained in their use.[21]

Hindess and Hirst depart from Althusser here in that they do not define the economy and its conditions of existence first, as an abstract concept, and then look at societies separately. Instead, they define the concept of the *economy* first and then consider the conditions of existence *only* as they really exist in concrete societies. They also stress, in a way that Althusser and Balibar do not, that economies cannot secure their *own* conditions of existence, since this would make them eternally self-reproducing. Conditions of existence are instead secured, modified, or transformed, by class struggles. In certain other respects, Hindess and Hirst follow Althusser. They indicate that societies can contain elements of other modes of production besides a dominant one, as long as the conditions of existence of the dominant mode are not thereby interfered with.

As I have indicated, the gain of Hindess and Hirst's work from the point of view of the analysis of ideology, is that it is a detailed consideration of the relationship between the economy and the ideological conditions of existence. To illustrate their method as sketched out above, I shall describe their account of economy and ideology in the slave mode of production, since this is one mode in which, according to them, ideology is dominant.

There is a distinction between slavery as an institution and slavery as a mode of production. Although the institution of slavery is basic to the mode of production, it is also compatible with other modes of production in a society. The first problem, therefore, is to work out the defining features of slavery as an institution. For Hindess and Hirst, the most important feature is that slavery is a *legal* form, not a relationship of *domination* between master and slave. The slave is the *property* of the master. 'The notion of the master-slave relation as a relation of domination between two subjects, as a personal duel of mastership and bondage, is a product of the age-old humanist myth that all social relations are in essence relations between human subjects.'[22]

Like any other mode, the slave mode of production has to be constituted by the articulation of the relations and forces of production. The relations of production in the slave mode have three levels. Firstly, there is a social division of labour into labourers and non-labourers, and there must be private property relations. As we have seen, the slaves are the private property of the masters. Secondly, masters must be able to put their slaves to work. Simple ownership of slaves is not enough; owners must also have raw materials, tools and the means of subsistence for the slave. So, in this mode, the labourers (slaves) are separated from the means of production which they neither possess nor own (see pp. 96–97 for elucidation of these concepts). Thirdly, the master appropriates the whole of the product. The master owns the product just as he owns the slave. In effect, unlike the labourer in capitalism, the slave is an element of capital for the master. In sum, 'in the SMP the mode of appropriation of the surplus-product is a function of the slave being the property of his owner. The three levels of the relations of production form a unity: the separation of the labourer from the means of production and his subsumption within capital make the product of the labourer the property of his owner.'[23]

As far as the forces of production are concerned, the most notable feature is a contradiction between the slave as a form of property and as a labourer. As a form of property, the slave is like fixed capital. He retains his value whether he labours or not, but he must be maintained whether he labours or not. Therefore, unlike the wage labourer in capitalism, the slave is not *forced* to sell his labour-power to provide for his own maintenance. The absence of any necessity to labour clearly creates a problem for the effective functioning of the slave mode. The problem is solved by a 'specific set of ideological practices' which are a necessary condition of existence of this mode. 'The nature of the agent's relation to the labour process is constituted by the ideological instance—it is this instance which forms the agents as subjects. . . . The slave may work through Christian religious duty, to serve God loyally in his station etc.'[24] The actual content of the ideological element is not deducible from the structure of the slave economy, but some such element is necessary.

Effectively, then, Hindess and Hirst give two ideological conditions of existence of the slave mode of production. Firstly, the slave is constituted as property by a legal system, and, secondly, there must be some way of relating the slave to the labour process so that he does perform productive labour. It should be clear that these ideological elements are treated as conditions of existence of the slave mode *only* because of the manner in which the concept of that mode is formulated.

Implications of the Concept of Mode of Production for the Analysis of Ideology

Despite some differences between writers on the notion of mode of production, there is still agreement that ideology should be seen as a condition of existence of the economy. This conception, even given the central importance that it is accorded, is still not precise enough. There needs to be some more clarification of certain points, the need for which is partly illustrated by a consideration of the arguments of Weber's *The Protestant Ethic and the Spirit of Capitalism.*[25] Despite the very general dislike of Weber's work displayed by most contemporary Marxists, there is a superficial similarity between his book and the arguments that I have been considering.

Weber is interested in the relationship of capitalism to certain ideological elements. He starts by defining a capitalistic economic action 'as one which rests on the expectation of profit by the utilization of opportunities for exchange, that is on (formally) peaceful chances of profit'.[26] Capitalism is not simple greed for gain, but is identical with the pursuit of profit by means of rationally organized enterprise. The key feature, which distinguishes 'true' capitalism from its later varieties, is its *rationality*. Weber then establishes his theoretical problem as being to explain the origins of capitalism with its rational organization of free labour. Or rather, and this is an important further step, the problem is to explain the origins of the Western bourgeois *class*. To anticipate rather, Weber's answer to his question lies in the peculiarly rationalistic quality of Western culture and, specifically, in the impact of the Protestant religions in the formation of that culture.

With this narrower delimitation of his problem, Weber's investigation takes the form of looking at the relationship between the kinds of beliefs and behaviour, especially rational action, which underpin capitalism, and the kinds of belief and behaviour involved in the Protestant religions. It is an investigation of the relation of the Protestant ethic and the spirit of capitalism. Quite simply, Weber argues that certain varieties of Protestantism were crucial in organizing their adherent's life into a rational whole. This was achieved by a variety of religious prescriptions, in favour of hard work and against the 'spontaneous enjoyment of life', in favour of man having a 'calling', and, in its more Calvinist forms, encouraging men to organize their lives so that their every action was a demonstration of their being one of God's elect. The 'Protestant ethic' so formed matched the forms of behaviour required for capitalist activity and provided, thereby, *one* of the essential preconditions for the emergence of capitalism. Ideology, in the form of Protestantism, is a precondition of capitalism.

In advancing such a claim, Weber rejects what he refers to as 'naive historical materialism', which would 'deduce the Reformation, as a historically necessary result, from certain economic changes',[27] a rejection similar to Althusser's opposition to vulgar and 'economistic' Marxism. At the same time, Weber does not want to go to the other extreme and endorse a 'spiritualistic' interpretation of history, which would insist that religious changes alone gave rise to the spirit of capitalism, or even, to capitalism as an economic system.

As far as the causal priority of economy and ideology in the form of religions is concerned, Weber has a clear, if indecisive, position. He rejects any assertion that economy *or* ideology have a causal primacy. The precise weight to be attached to either element in the explanation of historical change, however, cannot be determined *a priori*, but has, instead, to be settled by historical research. In this respect he clearly differs from Althusser and Hindess and Hirst, for they hold that the relations between economy and ideology *can* be constructed theoretically, even if one cannot thereby predict the precise character of any concrete society. In one other respect Weber's arguments differ from those that I have considered so far. He argues throughout his book that Protestantism is relevant only as a condition of existence of capitalism for the *origins* of capitalism. Once started, the *economic* structure of capitalism has a logic of its own which propels it along. 'The capitalistic economy of the present day is an immense cosmos into which the individual is born, and which presents itself to him . . . as an unalterable order of things in which he must live. It forces the individual, in so far as he is involved in the system of market relationships, to conform to capitalistic rules of action.' Any entrepreneur or worker who does not conform to this economic logic will soon be eliminated from the economic scene.

Weber, in stressing that the ethical maxims of Protestantism are not conditions 'of the further existence of present-day capitalism', again clearly differs from the theories of mode of production that we have considered, which suggest that the economy cannot work without the *continuous* intervention of ideology. Actually it is unclear, from this text of Weber, whether ideology *in some form* is not a condition of contemporary capitalism. This is not a question that directly interests Weber, for his own main concern is with the impact of Protestant religions, not with ideology in general. There are indications that he did think that the 'spirit of capitalism' was a continuing necessity. Thus 'the capitalistic system so needs this devotion to the calling of making money, it is an attitude toward material goods which is so well suited to that system, so intimately bound up with the conditions of survival in the economic struggle for existence . . .',[28] conceptions which seem to fit Althusser's definition of ideological practice very well. However, later in the same passage, Weber states clearly that, in established capitalism, 'Men's commercial and social interests do tend to *determine* their opinions and attitudes' (author's emphasis).

It may not be absolutely clear, therefore, what are Weber's views on the relationship between economy and ideology in contemporary capitalism. However, in emphasizing, again and again, the economic logic of capitalism and 'the fundamental importance of the economic factor', his work, in relation to that of Marxists, is intriguingly paradoxical. Weber, so often thought of as the opponent of Marxism, in fact emphasizes the economy, as an autonomous and basic set of practices, more than Althusser does.

It may not be entirely wise to compare Weber and Althusser too closely, if only because their philosophical and methodological preconceptions are so very different. Nonetheless, as I have indicated, Weber's work does raise the possibility that capitalism, as an economic structure, does not require ideology as a condition of its continuing existence. At the least, this casts doubt on the notion of condition of existence as *necessary*. To some extent, particularly for Althusser, this necessity is a creation of his epistemology. Since he insists on formulating the concept of a mode of production in the abstract, ideological conditions are conceptualized as abstract necessities. For Hindess and Hirst, this is less of a problem, since the ideological conditions of existence are conceptualized at the level of the concrete society, and their necessity does not appear to have the force of abstract reasoning. Nevertheless, for both sets of authors, the concept of condition of existence is conceived very strictly and the relationship between the conditions and the economy is very tight. Thus the economy *must* have conditions of existence, these conditions *must* be ideological and political, and the economy specifies what form the conditions take. Indeed the phrase 'necessary conditions of existence' conveys the sense almost of a logical, or internal conceptual relation, which is certainly what Althusser and Hindess and Hirst occasionally say. Because the concept of the economy entails the concept of specific conditions of existence, the relations between economy and ideology are conceptual ones. This conception of the conditions of existence is a very restricting one and its test might be to see if an economy is literally inconceivable without particular ideological structures. In Hindess and Hirst's analysis of the slave mode of production, for example, it is not only the case that there are ideological conditions of existence, the ideological structure is said to be dominant. But it is not clear why this *must* be the role of ideology or even why it should have any role at all. Let us suppose that they are correct in their analysis of the economy of slavery, that is that the constitution of the slave as property is vital and there is a contradiction between the slave as property and the slave as labourer, so that there is no compulsion to work. It is unclear why ideology is relevant here. Both rights of property and compulsion to work can be secured *politically* and, in the case of the latter, perhaps simply by the withholding of subsistence. Indeed it is not *literally* inconceivable that the economy could work without any ideological conditions of existence at all, even if it seems extremely *unlikely*, and it would be interesting to experiment with that possibility.

The discussion at this point has indicated that the relationship between economy and ideology has been drawn too tightly by utilizing the concept of condition of existence. More precision is needed here, including investigation of the possibility of looser relationships, such as ideology as 'helpful' at certain points. Such an investigation would have to include a careful specification of economic and ideological practices so that they are analytically separable. There is one other area in which greater precision would be an advantage. In a number of the accounts that I have discussed, ideology has a relationship to economy at many different levels. Ideology is said to underpin relationships of exchange, legitimate rights of property, and smooth over contradictions. Weber adds another dimension, for his discussion of the relation between ideology and the economy is effectively a theory of *motivation*; ideology is a requirement because it motivates a class of individuals to act in such a way that makes capitalist economic action possible. The problem is, that each of these different relations between economy and ideology has different theoretical implications. This is particularly true of the contrast between Weber's view and the others, as the notion of motivation makes certain assumptions about the relation of ideology to the individual human subject.

Social Classes and the Determination of Knowledge

The presentations of the concept of mode of production that I have discussed tend to go with a view of the human subject. Hindess and Hirst, for example, object to the 'reduction of social relations to effects of consciousness, or will, considered as natural attributes of human subjects'.[29] In a similar vein, Althusser says: '*the social relations of production are on no account reducible to mere relations between men*, to relations which only involve men. . . . For Marx, the social relations of production do not bring *men alone* onto the stage, but the *agents* of the production process . . . '.[30] Sociological analysis must not start with the intentions, dispositions or even actions of individuals, but instead with social relations as objective structures independent of the human subject. Human agency is not therefore a primary, but a derived, characteristic. As Marx says: 'the characters who appear on the economic stage are but the personifications of the economic relations that exist between them'.[31]

Such a view of human agents as merely the bearers of social relations spills over into the analysis of social class. In this field, it takes the form of objecting to the view that makes social class the primary and active element in society, that makes classes the 'subjects' or makers of history. Superficially, this is rather a surprising attitude. Marxism, as shown in Part I(1), is widely associated with an insistence on the importance of social classes. Further, Marx himself, in *The Communist Manifesto*, says that 'the history of all hitherto existing society is the history of class struggles'.[32]

This doctrine of the agency of social classes—or, rather, the lack of it—is represented in the work of another writer deeply influenced by Althusser, Poulantzas. Like Althusser, Poulantzas argues that social analysis cannot be reduced to inter-personal relations; individuals cannot be the 'origin of social action' or 'the genetic principle'. In a similar manner, social classes, being collections of individual human subjects, cannot be treated as the prime cause of social phenomena: 'social classes are never theoretically conceived by Marx as the genetic origin of structures, inasmuch as the problem concerns the definition of the concept of class'.[33] The difficulty then arises as to what is the theoretical status of social classes. Poulantzas's answer is that classes are *effects* of an underlying structure of social relations, to wit, the mode of production. He is careful to point out that classes are not produced by the economic structure alone, but by the economic, political and ideological structures conjointly. It is important to be clear what is being said here. The structure of the mode of production (in Althusser's sense) produces a particular distribution of agents into classes. It is the mode of production that has causal priority, not the social class. This is not to say that classes are without importance within this perspective. It will be remembered that

Hindess and Hirst give class-struggle a central place in their account of the transition from one mode of production to another. Poulantzas himself says, rather confusingly, that 'classes have existence only in the class struggle'.[34]

Such a view of social class must have profound implications for the practice of sociology in general,[35] since the subject takes the causal primacy of class very seriously. As far as the sociology of knowledge is concerned, most of the work reviewed in Part I of this book treats social class as a determinant of belief. Mannheim, in particular, took systems of belief as functions of social classes which were engaged in a struggle. One criticism of his work is that he did not explain where social classes came from, let alone why they struggled. Poulantzas scathingly refers to this kind of view as one which sees ideology as 'number-plates worn by social classes on their backs'.

One of the contrasts, therefore, between the approaches to the sociology of knowledge outlined in Parts I and II of this book, revolves round the treatment of class as a determinant of ideology. In the more conventional approach, class is primary, while in much contemporary Marxist work, the mode of production is central. I will borrow two terms from elsewhere to describe the two positions, class-theoretical and mode-theoretical. For the class-theoretical approach, ideologies are appropriate to classes (or, more generally, 'social positions') via the mechanism of class-interest. In the mode-theoretical view, ideology operates at the level of the mode of production as a condition of existence of the economy.

In part I(3), I presented an outline of an analysis of individualism and conservatism largely in terms of social classes having interests of particular kinds. Two interpretations of individualism are possible. Firstly, that set of doctrines suited the *economic* interests of a capitalist class because it made the economic practices of the class easier. Alternatively, individualism matched *political* interests because it made dissent from the feudal social order possible. The later decline in the importance of individualistic doctrines rather favours the second interpretation, in that it suggests that the capitalist class, having achieved dominance, has less need of doctrinal support for its dissent and, indeed, might find it a positive embarrassment. It is, furthermore, initially difficult to see how the economic practices of the bourgeoisie are supported by individualism in their early phase, but manage perfectly well without later on. However, the two interpretations are not incompatible and a theory might well be worked out which reconciled them. Thus a class-theoretical view is not totally impossible even if it is incomplete. In the examination of conservatism, I argued that rather more problems were presented by a class-theoretical account, for class-interest does not have the explanatory force that it has for the examination of individualism. In discussing Mannheim's analysis of conservatism, I argued that it is difficult to see why the aristocracy and the petit-bourgeioisie took up the particular *form* of belief that they did. An interest explanation is not particularly attractive, for it is unclear why, at this time, the economic interests of these social classes should produce conservative doctrines.

Would a mode-theoretical approach help in the resolution of these problems? One could perhaps show that individualism was an ideological condition of existence of the capitalist mode of production, possibly by developing the notion that individualism is a requirement for exchange and competition. Given such a demonstration, a mode-theoretical account could explain the subsequent decline of doctrines of individualism. As capitalism expands and develops, there is concentration and centralization of capital.[36] In turn, this process demands (as a condition of existence) the active and increasing involvement of the State. For such an involvement, the existence of individualistic doctrines of any kind is a positive impediment. Individualism becomes less relevant the more the State intervenes in the economy, taking over what had previously been *ideological* conditions of existence. As far as the analysis of conservatism is concerned, a great deal will depend on the theory of the relationships between modes of production or elements of modes of production. It will be remembered that Althusser sees societies as articulations of more than one mode of production. On such a view it would be necessary to see conservatism as an ideological condition of existence of a mode of production subordinate to capitalism, presumably feudalism, modified and influenced by the particular relationship between the modes.

A detailed re-investigation of individualism and conservatism is outside the scope of this book. However I hope that I have said enough to show that such an investigation is, at least, not an impossibility. There still remain, though, the problems, firstly, of whether the mode-theoretical account can say any more than a class-theoretical one, and, secondly, of what relationship there is between the two types of theory and between the concepts of mode and class.

Some light can be shed on these questions by a consideration of the more theoretical drawbacks of mode-theoretical approaches. Most basically, they have a tendency to *teleological argument,* in which it is unclear what the *mechanism* of a mode of production actually is. For example, in saying that there are ideological conditions of existence of an economy, one must be able to say how those conditions are secured. They cannot be secured automatically, or by the economy itself, for that would be a circular process without any apparent potential for change.[37] The notion that the mode of production somehow does things for itself, that it is an historical agent, is heavily criticized by Foster-Carter:

> much . . . work has tended to treat modes of production as entities occupying the totality of explanatory space—either omitting the political level (let alone others, such as the juridical or ideological), or relegating them to a minor and preordained place. The inevitable result is not only economism but reification. It is already one level of abstraction to have 'classes' (rather than 'people') as the subject of history; but to endow so conceptual an entity as 'mode of production' with this role is idealism indeed.

He suggests that the proper concern of the analysis of modes of production is to assist understanding of 'the material basis and workings of class alliances'.[38] It will be remembered that for Hindess and Hirst conditions of existence can be secured and maintained only by class-struggle. By such a view, they seek to avoid the teleological implications of the conception that the economy secures its own conditions of existence.

It is likely then, on a number of grounds, both substantive and theoretical, that any adequate mode-theoretical sociology of knowledge must grant a role to social classes. This would, by giving classes some mediating function, make the relationship between economy and ideology less tight and confining in the sense discussed above. In sum, the intention must be to avoid the defects of both extreme mode-theoretical and class-theoretical approaches. That is, there is no theoretical way of specifying the forms of belief taken up by social classes by reading those beliefs off from the characteristics of the dominant mode of production. This point is taken up again in the Conclusion.

6 HEGEMONY AND THE HUMAN SUBJECT

In this chapter I shall raise a number of problems posed by the contrast between the conventional approach to the sociology of knowledge outlined in Part I and its Marxist critique. In the last chapter, I talked of the possibility of a reconciliation between class-theoretical and mode-theoretical approaches, particularly as one may see ideological conditions of existence being secured by the actions of social classes. The concept of condition of existence is crucial to the mode-theoretical view of the sociology of knowledge, as I have outlined it, but it nonetheless contains an important ambiguity. In the last chapter, ideology was a condition of existence of the economy in the sense that it made the working of the economy possible, or at least easier. However ideology can also have the function of *concealing* the truth of the social world and, in particular, of preventing the subordinate classes perceiving their exploitation. Since the exploitation of the labourer is crucial to certain modes of production, capitalism for instance, this concealment could be said to be a condition of existence of the economy. It is important to stress how different are these two senses of ideological condition of existence. It is not that it is impossible to reconcile the two functions of ideology, only that they should be analytically separated. Indeed since, in Marxist theory at least, the two functions are often run together without explanation, it is important to have a well-worked-out theory of the connection between them.

While the first function of ideology (the 'mechanism' function) was largely dealt with in the last chapter, the second (the 'concealment' function) was discussed, in different forms, earlier on in the book. The account presented in Part I(1), for example, effectively equates the concealment function of ideology with the control of subordinate by dominant classes. In *The German Ideology*, Marx argues that the ruling class, in that they control 'the means of mental production', determine what ideas are diffused throughout society. Thus the ideas of the ruling class are the ruling ideas of every epoch. The fact of ideological control by the ruling class means that subordinate classes can think only within ruling class categories and literally lack the means of formulating their opposition. For example, an education system, the functioning of which is under the control of the ruling class, teaches all classes in society ways of thinking which support the political and economic position of the ruling class. I have argued that these arguments are seriously defective, both theoretically and substantively.[1] However, in themselves, they are also rather crude. From the point of view of the critique of contemporary Marxist writers, discussed in the last two chapters, a doctrine that emphasizes ideological control by a ruling class is class-theoretical, incorrectly placing class at the centre of analysis, and making the concealment function of ideology smack too much of 'one class doing something to another'. In addition, its view of concealment is simply that distorted beliefs are put about by the ruling class and contribute to a false consciousness in the working class. In this chapter I shall be investigating the concealment function of ideology particularly as it is explained by the conventional and critical Marxist approaches.

The Concept of Hegemony

I have earlier suggested that there is a certain tension within the classical Marxist theory of ideology.[2] On the one hand, Marx (and Engels even more so) emphasizes the way in which social classes have their 'own' systems of belief. This is so because classes have incompatible interests and very different life experiences determined by different positions in productive relations. On the other hand, Marx also argued that all social classes are incorporated within the *single* belief system which is appropriate to the interests of the dominant class. Within sociology generally, the second view has tended to predominate. That is, many sociologists have attributed the comparative stability of the capitalist social order, and the quiescence of the working class, to the fact that societies are permeated by an overarching system of values which ensures that all social classes hold the same beliefs and values. This emphasis on the integrating capacities of ideology is due, in some measure, to the work of Gramsci, an Italian Marxist, most of whose writing was done in prison in the twenties and thirties.[3] In taking such a view, Gramsci was reacting to the interpretations of Marxism prevalent at the time, which suggested that economic conditions were the only important object of analysis. Capitalism would necessarily collapse simply as a result of its internal economic contradictions. Ideology or class-consciousness, far from having any independent importance, was parasitic on economic position and would have no significant role in removing the capitalist class from its dominant place.

In formulating his theories, Gramsci's primary aim was to explain how the political and economic *supremacy* of particular social forces, classes, or class alliances, was secured and maintained. Generally, he argued, such a supremacy could not be created, let alone maintained, by force alone. Clearly, command of sufficient force is relevant, but so also is 'intellectual and moral leadership'. The actual balance of force and the ideological engineering of consent will vary from society to society. For example, Gramsci compares the East, where coercion exercised by the State is the dominant form of control, with the West, where moral persuasion is more important. However, in Gramsci's view, societies are more stable the more they attempt to obtain consent, and it is this process of establishing *hegemony* that commands most of his interest.

Hegemony, then, may be defined as 'an order in which a certain way of life and thought is dominant, in which one concept of reality is diffused throughout society, in all its institutional and private manifestations, informing with its spirit all tastes, morality, customs, religious and political principles, and all social relations, particularly in the intellectual and moral connotations'.[4] However, it should be clear that the establishment of consent is not merely a question of ruling groups *persuading* subordinate groups of the propriety of their rule. It also requires some compromise of the interests of all groups. Thus 'undoubtedly the fact of hegemony presupposes that account be taken of the interests and the tendencies of the groups over which hegemony is to be exercised, and that a certain compromise equilibrium be formed—in other words, that the leading group should make sacrifices of an economic—corporate kind.'[5] Hegemony, therefore, refers to a *number* of processes by which a ruling group obtains consent. But how is this achieved?

For an understanding of this question, a distinction between the concepts of civil society and political society is required. Civil society refers to those 'private' institutions which form society such as schools, churches or political parties, while political society refers to the 'public' organs of the State, the army, government and legal system. The relationship between state and civil society and their relative strengths, varies from society to society. Thus 'In Russia the State was everything, civil society was primordial and gelatinous; in the west, there was a proper relation between State and civil society, and when the State trembled, a sturdy structure of civil society was at once revealed. The State was only an outer ditch, behind which there stood a powerful system of fortresses and earthworks. . . .'[6] As Anderson[7] indicates, the predominance of civil society over political society in the West is intimately related to the importance of hegemony and consent, rather than coercion, as instruments of supremacy in capitalist societies. It is in civil society, rather than the State, that hegemony is generated; it is the education system, the churches and the mass-media that are the instruments of hegemony. If these private institutions are poorly developed in relation to the State, one must expect supremacy by coercion exercised by the organs of the State. This rather rigid distinction between civil society, the site of hegemony, and political society, the site of coercion, has its drawbacks however. In particular, it underestimates the degree to which the State itself is an instrument of hegemony as well as coercion. Partly, this is a question of some of the institutions of ideological dissemination being effectively parts of the State. As Gramsci himself says:

> Every State is ethical in so far as one of its most important functions is to elevate the great mass of the population to a given cultural and moral level, a level or standard which corresponds to the needs of development of the forces of production and

hence to the interests of the dominant classes. The school as a positive educational function and the courts as a negative and repressive educational function are the most important such activities of the State.[8]

However, as Anderson points out, the role of the State in winning consent is not limited to the activities of institutions like the legal or educational systems. The key to the problem lies in the *form* that the State takes in capitalist societies, namely parliamentary democracy, which is necessarily the very expression of consent. This form implies that every individual gives consent through his action as a voter. It may therefore be necessary to see hegemony, as the engineering of consent, as located in both civil society and political society.

Gramsci's view of ideology is, therefore, that it helps in eliciting the consent of subordinate classes in their domination. It must conceal the fact of domination or exploitation. It functions as a kind of 'cement', glueing elements of society together when they would otherwise fall apart. This image of ideology informs, in a somewhat different guise, the work of Althusser which will be reviewed later in this chapter. It has also influenced a number of Althusser's followers. Poulantzas, for example, suggests that Gramsci's metaphor of ideology as cement means that ideology hides the real contradictions and reconstitutes 'on an imaginary level a relatively coherent discourse which serves as the horizon of agents' experience'. He continues: 'Ideology, which slides into every level of the social structure, has the particular function of *cohesion*. It fulfils this function by establishing at the level of agents' experience relations which are obvious but false, and which allow their practical activities (division of labour, etc.) to function within the unity of a formation.'[9]

Within this conception of ideology as a cement which unifies a society, there is a clear risk of seeing societies as overintegrated, and of minimizing the degree of conflict. Gramsci attempts to avoid this danger, for he does not see hegemony as achieving perfect control of subordinate classes. In the discussion, in Part II(4) of Gramsci's notion of common-sense, I suggested that he saw working-class consciousness as being split. On the one hand, there is a consciousness determined by life-experiences and interests, which unites workers 'in the practical transformation of the real world'. Given the origin of this consciousness, it is implicitly oppositional. On the other hand, there is a whole tradition, a way of thinking, informed by the dominant culture, and 'uncritically absorbed'. Gramsci's suggestion is that the consciousness formed by workers' experience of life cannot by itself become radical or dominant because it is inherently fragmented. It cannot go beyond practical activity, for it has no *theoretical* component and, in fact, any theory that there is is provided by the dominant culture. Nonetheless, it will be clear from this that Gramsci holds that there is a certain resistance, founded in the workers' experience of their economic position within capitalism to complete incorporation within the dominant culture. The hegemony of the capitalist class is not complete because the consent given by workers is not wholehearted, even if their opposition is not developed either.

The suggestion about the incompleteness of hegemony prompts questions about how hegemony is overthrown, and how the supremacy of one social class passes to another. Gramsci is clear that a social force only comes to power if it has already demonstrated the capacity to 'lead'. This capacity is made up of two elements. Firstly, a dominant group must be able to organize and lead its allies, and secondly, it must have already established its intellectual hegemony. 'A social group can, and indeed must, already exercise "leadership" before winning governmental power (this indeed is one of the principal conditions for the winning of such power); it subsequently becomes dominant when it exercises power, but even if it holds it firmly in its grasp, it must continue to "lead" as well.'[10] Ideological supremacy is thus a *precondition* for the successful seizure of power, and, although Gramsci was interested mainly in showing how this was historically true of domination by the capitalist class, as in the Risorgimento in Italy, he also believed that it applied to the transformation to socialism.

As we have seen from Gramsci's account of common-sense, cultural hegemony is *theoretical*, by contrast with the unorganized quality of common-sense. Ruling groups, in establishing hegemony, therefore require the services of practitioners, intellectuals, specializing in the construction of systems of thought. So also do oppositional groups, seeking to secure *their* hegemony, need a class of intellectuals. In particular, a revolutionary socialist party must attempt to radicalize the consciousness of the working class by providing an intellectual justification of socialism that can counter the dominant culture.

Such a view of the party, and of the role of intellectuals within the party, implies a more general theory about the relative independence of intellectual knowledge of the economy, and of its independent function in promoting economic change. This is an account of the relation between base (or structure) and superstructure very like that of Engels as presented in Part I(A). For Gramsci, not only do ideas have their own laws of development, they also affect the base. They cannot be simply 'read off' from an analysis of the economy. There is a 'necessary reciprocity between structure and superstructure, a reciprocity which is nothing other than the real dialectical process'.[11] In a very different way, Gramsci also believed, not only in the relative autonomy of ideology as a *structure* of ideas, but also in the way that classes act, independently of any economic determination, to change their circumstances, and even in the way that particular individuals could have historical significance. Thus he not only held to the autonomy of ideas but also to the autonomy of human individuals and class-subjects.

The Critique of the Classical View of the Dominant Ideology

Gramsci undoubtedly offers a more sophisticated theory of the concealment or control function of ideology than the conventional view outlined at the beginning of this chapter. However he still operates within the methodological ambit of that view, especially as his account is class-theoretical. Indeed, on occasions, his writing reads rather like that of Mannheim, in the central place it gives to class forces, class-struggle, and the establishment of supremacy.

In the last two chapters I have been outlining a number of criticisms of the conventional account of the sociology of knowledge, as they appear from a Marxist perspective. In the last chapter, I considered the critique of theories of what I have called the mechanism function of ideology, in which ideology is said to help or promote the economic behaviour of individuals. A critique of conventional theories of the *concealment* function of ideology, in which ideology conceals the truth of exploitation and hence makes control by the dominant class much easier, will follow the same critical methodological principles. Two such principles would be important. Firstly, concealment must refer, not to simple distortion or falsity of belief, but to the way in which beliefs represent 'real' relations which also conceal. Secondly, pride of theoretical place must go to *structures* of social relations, rather than to social classes or human individuals. The theory of commodity fetishism looks as though it might be an alternative to conventional views of the concealment function. This theory suggests, it will be remembered, that commodities appear as things exchanged in a market, an appearance that conceals the reality of the relations of production. Further, as Callinicos points out:

> Thus fetishism is not simply an illusory appearance. It is the mode of existence of capitalist production. The mystified character of the system results not from some accidental feature of it, or from the skill of the capitalists in fooling workers, but from its very heart, from the nature of the commodity, that is, from the very form that the products of labour must take under the capitalist mode of production.[12]

However, as I have noted in Part II(4), the theory of fetishism, as a complete theory of ideology, has its problems, problems that relate to the very methodological principles outlined above. Amongst other things, the theory is too restrictive as to the kinds of belief that can be analysed, it does not allow for the existence of illusory beliefs, and it seems to demand, for its completeness, some account of the role of social classes.

Given Althusser's general position, one would have expected him to produce a theory of the concealment function of ideology of a critical kind, similar in methodological intent to his analysis of the mechanism function. Thus Hirst describes Althusser's conception of ideology as rejecting 'the conception of ideologies as reflections of social reality in consciousness and the substitution of a conception of ideology as a structure of social relations no less "real" than the economic . . .'. Further, 'the social position of the subject is not the origin of its ideological position; ideology has conditions of existence which cannot be "read off" from the place of the subject in the relations of production'.[13] At the same time, in his later work, Althusser is trying to correct certain of his earlier principles that he feels may have been over stated. In particular, he tries to rectify his neglect of the class-struggle. In his essay 'Ideology and Ideological Stage Apparatuses',[14] for example, Althusser wishes to conceive of ideology as a site of class-struggle. Indeed it has been argued that Althusser has three views of ideology, which can be more or less represented as stages in the development of his theory.[15] Firstly, he conceives of ideology as a structure, or instance, equivalent in theoretical status to the political and economic, and functioning as a condition of existence of the economy. Secondly, ideology is seen as an epistemological category, in contrast to science. Thirdly, ideology is some kind of medium, whereby men are related to their world. The first and second senses have already been discussed in other parts of this book. As far as the analysis of ideological concealment is concerned, it is the sense of ideology as a medium that is relevant.

The Ideological State Apparatuses and the Human Subject

Althusser starts his analysis of the concealment function of ideology by considering the importance of the reproduction of the conditions of production. That is, economies, if they are to last any length of time, must not only produce, they must also renew all that is necessary to continue production. Specifically, that means the continuous renewal (reproduction) of (1) the productive forces and (2) the existing relations of production. In turn, the reproduction of the productive forces means the reproduction of the means of production (buildings, tools and machines) and the reproduction of labour-power. The first of these is comparatively uncontroversial. However, as far as the renewal of labour-power is concerned, it should be noted that that not only includes the material requisites of life—housing, food and clothing—but it also includes provision for keeping the labour-force 'competent', 'i.e. suitable to be set to work in the complex system of the process of production'.[16] Thus, as modern production techniques become more complex, a higher level of technical skill is required. Generally, in contemporary capitalist societies, the acquisition of such skills takes place in school or college rather than 'on the job'. However schools not only teach technical skills, they also instil the 'rules of good behaviour', that is, 'the rules of the established order i.e. a reproduction of submission to the ruling ideology for the workers, and a reproduction of the ability to manipulate the ruling ideology correctly for the agents of exploitation and repression, so that they, too, will provide for the domination of the ruling class "in words".'[17]

Since, for Althusser, the relations of production are also crucial for the functioning of the economy (see Part II(5)), they too must be reproduced. That is, the relations of domination required for the extraction of surplus-value and the relations of ownership and possession must be preserved.

How, then, is the reproduction of the relations of production (and of the 'rules of good behaviour') secured, given that the reproduction of the other elements of the conditions of production seems fairly straightforward? Althusser's answer is that it is secured by the 'legal-political and ideological superstructure' and, more precisely, by two apparatuses of the State, the Repressive State Apparatus and the Ideological State Apparatus. Althusser defines these two apparatuses essentially by giving a list of the institutions of which they are composed. Thus the Repressive State Apparatus (hereafter RSA) consists of the government, the civil service, the army, the police, the judiciary and the prisons. The Ideological State Apparatus (hereafter ISA) is made up of religious and educational institutions, the apparatuses of political parties and trade unions, radio, television and the press, artistic and recreational institutions, and the family. There is therefore only one RSA, whose elements are centrally organized, but a multiplicity of ISAs, which are relatively autonomous of one another. Those institutions that Althusser has grouped together as ISAs are all 'private' organizations and it is not clear why they are supposed to be part of, and organized by, the State. Althusser's defence of his position is not very convincing, and it seems as misguided to suggest that ideological dissemination is uniquely a property of the State, as it is for Gramsci to argue that it is never part of the State.

In any event, the critical difference between ISAs and RSAs lies in the functions that they perform. Not surprisingly, ISAs function largely by ideology, although they will also use repression in certain circumstances, as when, for example, the Church or the school uses punishment, or the press uses censorship. Similarly, the RSA functions primarily by repression, although it will also utilize ideology, as when the police or army require ideological cohesion. In capitalism the ISAs are more important directly in the reproduction of the relations of production. As Althusser says:

> . . . above all, the State apparatus secures by repression . . . the political conditions for the action of the Ideological state Apparatuses. In fact, it is the latter which largely secure the reproduction specifically of the relations of production, behind a 'shield' provided by the repressive State apparatus. It is here that the role of the ruling ideology is heavily concentrated, the ideology of the ruling class, which holds State power. It is the intermediation of the ruling ideology which ensures a (sometimes teeth-gritting) 'harmony' between the repressive state apparatus and the Ideological State Apparatus, and between the different State Ideological Apparatuses.[18]

Societies differ in the relations of RSA and ISAs and in the kinds of ISA present. For example, in the pre-capitalist period there was one dominant ISA, namely the Church, which included within its functions educational and cultural elements, which have since become separated out into other ISAs. This incidentally explains why the bourgeoisie were so violently anti-clerical in the French Revolution. They perceived the importance of the Church in the maintenance of feudal relations of production. In capitalist societies, however, the educational system is the dominant ISA; '. . . no other ideological state apparatus has the obligatory (and not least, free) audience of the totality of the children in the capitalist social formation, eight hours a day for five or six days out of seven'.[19]

Althusser's theory of ISAs is very like the classical theory of the concealment function of ideology and is, particularly, like Gramsci's variant of the classical theory. For Gramsci, ideological hegemony is a condition of the continued supremacy of the bourgeoisie, while for Althusser, the Ideological State Apparatuses are the most important means by which existing relations of production are perpetuated and 'submission to the rules of the established order' ensured. For both, ideologies conceal and hence control. Indeed Althusser's theoretical debt to Gramsci is considerable, not only in the formulation of the concept of the ISA, but also in the relationship between the RSA and the ISAs. In this similarity to Gramsci's position, Althusser is, however, departing somewhat from his own principles. Firstly, a great deal of the analysis in the 'Ideology and Ideological State Apparatuses' article has the tone of the class-theoretical approach. Thus Althusser falls into a way of talking which makes it as if a ruling class was using ideology as a weapon of subjection; ideology is somehow an *instrument* creating a mystified consciousness. Thus Althusser speaks of ideologies as invariably expressing class positions and suggests, bluntly, that 'no class can hold State power over a long period without at the same time exercising its hegemony over and in the State Ideological Apparatuses'.[20] Secondly, Althusser implies that ideologies do have a distorting effect rather than representing 'real' social relations. Thirdly, the analysis of the ISAs is economistic in that Althusser derives the importance and content of ideology from the economy, primarily in terms of the necessity for the reproduction of relations of production.

In Hirst's view, Althusser is slipping back into the classical formulations from which his earlier work on ideology was trying to escape. Althusser is tending to a 'vulgar materialism' in which 'classes as social forces are directly constituted by the economic structure, their "interests" are given independently of ideological and political practice and their political and ideological representatives are directly determined by the economic.'[21] From Althusser's point of view, however, his newer views are an attempt to redress certain problems generated by his earlier theories of ideology. One effect of these changes is to relate social classes to the more general analysis of mode of production. As I have indicated in previous chapters, the mode-theoretical approach has certain tensions within it which necessitates some alteration in the general direction in which Althusser is going.[22]

Any assessment of Althusser's theory of Ideological State Apparatuses must take into account the context in which it is set.

This is that Althusser wishes to advance what he calls a theory of ideology 'in general'. It is unfortunate that his views on this question are very difficult, presented in the form of notes, and have an uncertain relation to the theory of ISAs.

Althusser emphasizes that ideology is a 'lived relation'. People live in ideological forms and it is in this sense that they are 'real'. For example, it is impossible to live in capitalist society without being involved in wage-labour which is a real relation. However it is also an ideological form since it conceals the underlying relations involved in the extraction of surplus-value. Ideology is therefore the form in which men relate to their world. In this sense, no society can be without ideology. Thus Althusser says, 'Human societies secrete ideology as the very element and atmosphere indispensable to their historical respiration and life,'[23] and, more specifically, 'ideology (as a system of mass representations) is indispensable in any society if men are to be formed, transformed, and equipped, to respond to the demands of their conditions of existence'.[24] The necessity of ideology applies to all societies, including classless ones. However, in class society, ideology is the means by which the relation between men and their 'conditions of existence' is resolved to the benefit of the dominant classes, while in classless societies, it is the means by which that relation benefits all men.

The ideological *form* of the relation between men and their conditions of existence is 'imaginary'. Ideology does not, as one might expect, reveal the real and most fundamental nature of that relation. More precisely, ideology does not represent (or distort) the real conditions of existence, for example the relations of production, but does represent the *relation* of individuals to those relations. Because only the *relation* of individuals to their conditions of existence is represented in ideology, the nature of the conditions of existence themselves is obscured, and it is in this sense that ideology is 'imaginary'. Thus, 'What is represented in ideology is therefore not the system of the real relations which govern the existence of individuals, but the imaginary relation of those individuals to the real relations in which they live.'[25] Althusser is therefore proposing a formulation like those discussed in Part II(A). Ideology refers to real relations which nevertheless conceal. It is unfortunate that Althusser is not very precise on this point and the doctrine remains a little obscure. As an example, he takes the 'humanist ideology' of equality, freedom and reason of the eighteenth century. The promulgation of these doctrines by a bourgeoisie was not deliberately intended cynically to deceive. The bourgeoisie had to believe in freedom not only to deceive more effectively, but because freedom of this kind is necessary for its economic practice. For the bourgeoisie 'freedom' represents a lived relation to economic practice. For the worker, freedom is also a lived relation since, in capitalism, he is a free labourer, unconstrained by feudal ties, and formally able to sell his labour-power to whosoever he chooses. Nonetheless, the worker's freedom has an imaginary character, since it conceals his exploitation in the very act of selling his labour-power. 'Thus, in a very exact sense, the bourgeoisie *lives* in the ideology of *freedom* the relation between it and its conditions of existence: that is, its real relation (the law of a liberal capitalist economy) *but invested in an imaginary relation* (all men are free, including the free labourers).'[26] In itself this example is an ingenious one, if only because it shows a way of reconciling the mechanism with the concealment function of ideology; an element of ideology is a condition of existence of the economic practice of capitalism and also functions to conceal the relations of production. Nevertheless, it is not entirely clear how it illustrates the general doctrine of ideology as an imaginary relation, particularly as it does not show what Althusser means by the *relation* to the conditions of existence themselves.

So far, we are given an account of the quality of ideology as an imaginary relation. There is still the question of how it achieves its effect. Althusser's answer is that ideology works only because of the category of the subject; 'the category of the subject is only constitutive of all ideology insofar as all ideology has the function (which defines it) of "constituting" concrete individuals as subjects'.[27] The process by which individuals are instituted as subjects is 'interpellation' or hailing which, Althusser suggests, is like any casual hailing in the street. Any person hailed, who turns round, becomes a subject because 'he has recognized that the hail was "really" addressed to him, and that "it was really him (sic) who was hailed" (and not someone else).'[28] Ideology thus 'fixes' individuals, and gives them a place as subjects in a particular set of social processes. Althusser's comments on this topic are very schematic and represent only the beginnings of a theory of the way that ideology constitutes individuals as subjects. Further developments may depend on the use of the findings of other disciplines, such as psychoanalysis and linguistics, which would recognize the crucial role of language in the interpellation of the subject.[29]

The Mechanism of Transmission

One area generally neglected by the sociology of knowledge, both conventional and critical, is that of the methods by which ideology is transmitted. The conventional theory of the concealment function of ideology clearly needs to be able to show how the ruling class is able to transmit its beliefs in such a way that they become incorporated as components of working-class consciousness. Similarly, the critical theory requires an account of how it is that ideologies are distributed in societies, even if the machinery of distribution is not seen as being at the service of a dominant class. Indeed, I have criticized the critical theory itself for implying that ideology appears almost by itself without any institutional mediation.

Conventionally, the problem of transmission is recognized as a problem of *intellectuals*—it is the intellectual stratum that articulates and gives shape to bodies of belief, and is then also responsible for their transmission to society at large.[30] There are two extreme views of the position of intellectuals. Firstly, they are seen as an autonomous grouping without any strict social ties with other groups. This autonomy gives them a commanding position since their intellectual constructions are then also independent and and not beholden to the interests of other social forces. In the second view, intellectuals are seen as more or less tied to social classes articulating the interests of those classes. Intellectuals are then simply class-spokesmen. Mannheim, it will be remembered, adopted both these points of view, as well as other intermediate ones, at various times in his career. Thus, in his *Ideology and Utopia* he formulated (or borrowed) the notion of the 'unattached intelligentsia', able to synthesize the viewpoints of competing social classes. In his essay on 'Conservative Thought' on the other hand, he thought of the Romantic writers as spokesmen for the aristocracy.

Shils advocates a position rather like that of Mannheim's unattached intellectuals. He starts from the position that all societies have needs of an intellectual or spiritual kind. That is, there is a need for 'contact with the sacred', for art of various forms, for contact with the past, for educationalists and administrators, and lastly for 'some sense of the stability, coherence, and orderliness of their society' expressed 'by a body of symbols, such as songs, histories, poems, biographies, constitutions, etc. which diffuse a sense of affinity among the members of the society'.[31] The activities of ordinary life do not permit any intellectual activity which might meet these societal needs for it is necessarily dedicated to the 'here and now'. However, fortunately, in every society, there is a minority of men who, naturally, have an inquiring turn of mind and are able to 'penetrate beyond the screen of immediate concrete experience'. The product of a societal need and a group of suitable persons, is a specialized group of intellectuals.

The function of the intellectual stratum is to articulate and mould the body of values central to a society and to provide for the laity 'a means of participation in the central value system'. However, it is not only a question of preserving and transmitting the traditional culture. Intellectuals also have the duty of deepening and extending it. This latter duty carries with it the risk of the active reformulation, or even rejection, of the central value system. Some intellectuals, therefore, may be promulgating the dominant values, while others will espouse oppositional beliefs, simply as a function of the nature of intellectual activity. Therefore, intellectuals can have any kind of relation to other groupings in society and Shils documents their attachment both to authorities and to subordinate groups.

Shils's analysis leaves a good deal to be explained, particularly as to the theoretical status of the need that societies have for the products of intellectuals. Most importantly, however, his account is curiously unsociological. Thus a particular body of intellectual ideas, or changes in such ideas, tend to be explained by reference to the ideas themselves. The rejection of prevailing knowledge or belief is intrinsic to intellectual activity itself. Intellectual dissent is

a product of the battle of ideas or, at most, a battle between intellectuals. Intellectual activity then appears as an autonomous
practice which may become attached to social forces. For example,
Shils, in his analysis of British intellectuals after the war, notes that
they have adopted a version of aristocratic culture, which, amongst
other things, praises all things British. This is in marked contrast to
intellectual life before the war which was abrasive, dissenting and
certainly anti-aristocratic. However this change in perspective is
analysed at the cultural level only, and there is little reference to
any social change which might explain it. Intellectual dissent, or the
lack of it, has little relation to other kinds of dissent.

Clearly, implicit in a good deal of sociology of knowledge, and,
especially to that at all influenced by Marx, there will be a much
tighter notion of the relationship between the intellectual stratum
and other social forces. Gramsci, it will be recalled, gives intellectuals a crucial place in the relationship between consciousness
and society. In his view, everyone is an intellectual in some sense, in
that everybody works out some conception of the world or has a
'conscious line of moral conduct'. In addition, any task, however
menial, requires creative intellectual activity of some kind.
However, 'All men are intellectuals, one could therefore say: but
not all men have in society the function of intellectuals.'[32] There are
therefore specialized groups of intellectuals, specialized by the
function that they perform, and intellectual only in the sense that
they have made a profession of a quality inherent in all men and
women. It is not the activity that makes an intellectual, but the
function.

Gramsci made it quite clear that there is no autonomous intellectual stratum. There is no such thing as intellectual activity
without some relationship to social activity. Furthermore, in his
view, every intellectual group was attached to some social class.
'Every social group, coming into existence on the original terrain of
an essential function in the world of economic production, creates,
together with itself, organically, one or more strata of intellectuals
which give it homogeneity and an awareness of its own function,
not only in the economic, but also in the social and political
fields.'[33] The relationship between intellectuals and social classes
is not, therefore, one in which the former perform *technical*
functions for the latter. Intellectuals are most important in that they

articulate the view of the social world appropriate to a social class. However, intellectuals are not all related in the same way to social classes. There are groups 'organically' bound to a social class because they have been more or less created by the same social process that produced the social class, and they may represent 'specializations of partial aspects of the primitive activity of the new social type which the new class has brought into prominence'.[34] There are also groups, 'traditional' intellectuals, which are less bound to dominant social classes. These intellectuals are effectively survivors of a previous epoch, in which they were organic to the then dominant class. Gramsci gives, as an example, the ecclesiastics of the Catholic Church who were, in feudal times, organically bound to the landed aristocracy, but have survived the disappearance of feudalism through their 'esprit de corps' and their 'special qualification'. Such groups may *believe* that they are autonomous, but, Gramsci argues, such a belief is utopian, though not without interest since it is the foundation of idealist philosophy in which ideas have the primary role in social life rather than material factors. Even traditional intellectuals are necessarily involved with the dominant classes, even if less so than the organic group. In sum: 'An independent class of intellectuals does not exist, but rather every social group has its own intellectuals. However, the intellectuals of the historically progressive class . . . exercise such a power of attraction that they end . . . by subordinating the intellectuals of the social groups and thus create a system of solidarity among all intellectuals. . . .'[35]

For Gramsci, although intellectuals might well be tied to social classes, they are still of crucial importance, for they articulate the world-view of social classes, where that would otherwise remain unorganized. For the dominant classes, they provide an intellectual and moral hegemony, which is, as we have seen, of fundamental importance. For the subordinate classes, intellectuals can mobilize and form the aspirations and beliefs that are present within common-sense thinking. Clearly it will not do merely to assert that there is a relatively tight relationship between intellectuals and classes. There has to be a detailed specification of the mechanism of the relationship. Following Mannheim, such a specification might well have to take the form of studying the intellectual group as a *partly* independent factor that may make its own contribution in articulating the world-view of a class. Thus, as Nettl points out,[36] it might be wise to see ideas as produced first and then coming to have a functional relationship with a social class.

As I have suggested, focus on the intellectual group exclusively tends to produce analysis which dissociates intellectuals from society and which makes dissent a purely intellectual matter. Furthermore, discussion of intellectuals within the conventional sociology of knowledge reflects the concern of that approach with intellectual knowledge, rather than those categories of belief discussed at the beginning of Part II(4).

Analysis of intellectuals as producers of specialist knowledge, or as class-spokesmen is undoubtedly valuable. However, again, one should be wary of narrowing the focus too much, for, as far as the transmission of belief is concerned, institutions (or apparatuses) are of far more significance, especially in capitalist societies, and intellectuals are usually located in, and constrained by, these institutions. Therefore, any developed sociology of knowledge has to incorporate studies of educational institutions, the Church, the mass-media, political parties and trade unions, inasmuch as these are all apparatuses of transmission of belief.

III
The Critique from Phenomenology

7 SCHUTZ

The phenomenological critique of orthodox sociology of knowledge has two main elements. There is, firstly, the feeling that orthodox sociology is unreal and artificial, and quite fails to come to grips with the 'real' social world. One of the reasons for the alleged unreality of sociology is that it fails to analyse the everyday world in which people live. The fault is not because sociology (and especially the sociology of belief) studies intellectuals and intellectualized beliefs, rather than the man in the street, but rather that sociologists seem uninterested in the ordinary, routine practices that all human beings engage in every day. The problem is that the reality of everyday life is taken for granted by everybody, since everybody, including sociologists, participates in it. The very fact that it is routine means that it is scientifically unsurprising. However, this conceals the manner in which everyday life is a *constructed* reality, which has to be constantly maintained.

Secondly, there is a general dislike of what are seen to be the deterministic assumptions about human nature implicitly, or explicitly, made by orthodox sociology and carried over into the sociology of knowledge. It is felt that man is seen as ensnared in social structures which mould him and determine what he will do. The suggestion is that orthodox sociology has a picture of man born into a world over which he has no real control; society is something that *does* things to people. The phenomenological solution is to replace this essentially passive view of mankind with a view that stresses man's autonomy in creating his social world. As Speier argues:

> Human subjectivity is an active, creative force in the con-
> stitution of the real world. The human mind is not a passive
> receptor of an independently and pre-formed order of
> meaningful events. Meaning is not found in objects or events as
> a self-originating property; rather it is constituted . . . Social
> reality is constructed by persons in everyday life. . . .[1]

Clearly these two elements of critique are closely related.
Everyday life is the fundamental reality and it is one constructed by
active, autonomous, human agents. This view has implications for
the nature of sociology as a scientific practice. If in conventional
sociology men are seen as determined by social structures, then one
could adopt the view that sociology is a science with methods and
procedures not, in principle, different from those of the natural
sciences. If, on the other hand, man is seen as a creative and
meaning-endowing creature, whose social behaviour originates in
his consciousness, then a rigid distinction between the natural and
social worlds can be made, with the consequent belief that
sociology cannot be scientific in the same way that, for example,
physics can be. This is the crux of the difference between conventional sociology (including the sociology of knowledge) and the
phenomenological school, a difference lying in the very basic
debate about what kind of enterprise sociology is supposed to be.

There are actually difficulties in constructing a school of
phenomenological socioligists who would all have common interests beyond an insistence on the priority of the world of
common-sense. In particular, the depth of opposition to orthodox
sociology varies considerably. Some writers argue, for example,
that a reconciliation is possible between phenomenology and
conventional sociology.[2] Others would suggest that conventional
sociology is beyond repair and that a dedicated interest in the
construction of the everyday world rules out any analysis that
refers to social *structures*.[3] In my analysis of phenomenological
sociology of knowledge I am going to confine myself to the work of
three writers, Schutz, Luckmann and Berger, who are all closely
linked.

Schutz was primarily a phenomenological philosopher, interested in extending and refining the earlier work of Husserl. His
work is often not of a directly sociological character or, perhaps

more precisely, is not incorporated in a sociological debate. From a sociological point of view, therefore, it is a question of extracting a sociology out of Schutz's writings, and from the narrower perspective of the sociology of knowledge, Schutz is best seen in his influence on the work of Berger and Luckmann.

Schutz, as sociologist, was interested in three problems. Firstly, he wanted to construct an adequate theory of social action, partly based on a critique of Weber.[4] Secondly, he carried out a series of investigations into the constitution of the 'life-world',[5] and, thirdly, he tried to deal with the scientificity of a sociology which took action and the life-world as important, if not basic, topics.[6] These three interests are directly connected since, in order to understand how men act in their everyday lives, it is necessary to understand how they interpret the everyday world in which they act. This necessity for 'subjective interpretation' forces a certain method on social scientists, for they 'always *can*—and for certain purposes *must*—refer to the activities of the subjects within the social world and their interpretation by the actors in terms of systems of projects, available means, motives, relevances, and so on'.[7] However, such a method appears to cast doubt on the status of sociology, as an objective and scientific discipline, for, as Schutz asks, 'How is it, then, possible to grasp by a system of objective knowledge subjective meaning structures?'[8] Schutz's project is, therefore, to work out a reconciliation of the phenomenological concentration on the intentions and purposes of the human actor with some conception of objective social science.

The Knowledge of the Life-world

'The sciences that would interpret and explain human action and thought must begin with a description of the foundational structures of what is prescientific, the reality which seems self-evident to men remaining within the natural attitude. This reality is the everyday life-world.'[9] Schutz sees the everyday life-world as something normally taken-for-granted, a world which may pose problems, but which is at least not systematically threatening. 'It is the unexamined ground of everything given in my experience, as it were, the taken-for-granted frame in which all the problems which

I must overcome are placed. The world appears to me in coherent arrangements of well-circumscribed objects having determinate properties.'[10] The life-world thus appears as a rather bland place, unthreatening, coherent, and unquestioned. It was here before our birth and will be here after our death. This blandness of tone gives a peculiarly conservative tone to much of Schutz's writings, a tone which has found its way into much of the work of Schutz's successors.

However, the everyday world is not simply a collection of objects. It consists, very importantly of other people with whom we have relationships of various kinds; it is 'intersubjective'. It is also characterized by our attempts to intervene in it, to manipulate it, or 'work' on it, in accordance with our interests. Schutz sums up the 'cognitive style' of the world of everyday life as follows:

(1) a specific tension of consciousness, namely wide-awakeness, originating in full attention to life; (2) a specific epoché, namely suspension of doubt; (3) a prevalent form of spontaneity, namely working (a meaningful spontaneity based upon a project and characterized by the intention of bringing about the projected state of affairs by bodily movements gearing into the outer world); (4) a specific form of experiencing one's self (the working self as the total self); (5) a specific form of sociality (the common intersubjective world of communication and social action); (6) a specific time-perspective. . . .[11]

The everyday world so defined is the paramount reality, the one in which we live most of our lives. However, there are other worlds, or 'provinces of meaning' as Schutz calls them, the worlds of dreams, of religious experience, of science, or of the insane, for instance. Each of these provinces has its own peculiar cognitive style, which gives coherence to experiences within the province. However, the very specificity of a cognitive style to a province of meaning, means that each province is relatively insulated from every other. Schutz suggests that passages from one province of meaning to another can occur only by means of a cognitive leap which is perceived as some kind of shock.

The knowledge appropriate to the everyday life-world is of different kinds. Firstly, there is basic knowledge, basic because it is intrinsic to human nature and does not, therefore, vary between social situations. For example, I know whether or not something is within my reach. Of much greater interest, however, is that kind of knowledge that does vary from one social situation to another. Of this category, most important for Schutz is knowledge that he calls routine, in turn divided into habitual, useful, and recipe knowledge. These three kinds of knowledge can be arranged on a continuum by the degree to which one has to *attend* when exercising them. Habitual knowledge, an example of which is the ability to walk, does not require active attention, while recipe knowledge, such as a hunter's skill in reading tracks, does. However it is recipe knowledge that is most typical of the *everyday* life world and is most significant in mastering everyday situations, and Schutz has probably inspired more empirical work in this area than any other. I would like to give a long quotation from Schutz's *Collected Papers* which gives a good idea of the importance of recipe knowledge.

Apparently there is a kind of organization by habits, rules, and principles which we regularly apply with success. But the origin of our habits is almost beyond our control; the rules we apply are rules of thumb and their validity has never been verified. The principles we start from are partly taken over uncritically from parents and teachers, partly distilled at random from specific situations in our lives or in the lives of others without our having made any further inquiry into their consistency. Nowhere have we a guarantee of the reliability of all of these assumptions by which we are governed. On the other hand, these experiences and rules are sufficient to us for mastering life. As we normally have to act and not to reflect in order to satisfy the demands of the moment, which it is our task to master, we are not interested in the 'quest for certainty'. We are satisfied if we have a fair chance of realizing our purposes, and this chance, so we like to think, we have if we set in motion the same mechanism of habits, rules and principles which formerly stood the test and which still stand the test. Our knowledge in daily life is not without hypotheses, inductions, and predictions, but they all have the character of the approximate and the typical. The ideal of everyday knowledge is not certainty, nor even probability in a mathematical sense, but just likelihood. Anticipations of future states of affairs are conjectures about what is to be hoped or feared, or at best about what can be reasonably expected. When afterwards the anticipated state of affairs takes some form in actuality, we do not say that our prediction has come true or proved false, or that our hypothesis has stood the test, but that our hopes or fears were or were not well founded. The consistency of this system of knowledge is not that of natural laws, but that of typical sequences and relations.

This kind of knowledge and its organization I should like to call 'cook-book knowledge'. The cook-book has recipes, lists of ingredients, formulae for mixing them, and directions for finishing off. This is all we need to make an apple pie and also all we need to deal with the routine matters of daily life.[12]

The Structure of the Stock of Knowledge

The stock of knowledge of the everyday life-world is not some loose and random jumble of items. On the contrary, it is essentially organized. Our knowledge of the world is arranged in a series of zones from that that is within 'actual reach' to zones of 'restorable and attainable reach'.[13] All these zones have a temporal and, most importantly, social structure.

The centre of everybody's life-world is himself or herself; the zones of temporally and socially structured knowledge are grouped around the self as centre. Closest to the self is the zone of 'directly experienced social reality'. Persons who come within my direct experience domain share a community of space and a community of time with me. I am aware of such people as *particular* individuals and I can share their subjective experiences. The zone of direct experience is thus vivid, with each perception being unique. Schutz does not say so, but people of whom we have direct experience are obviously those that we know well, whether they are family or friends. However it is not exactly the depth of the knowledge of others that interests Schutz, but its quality; direct experience is *unique* experience.

Outside the zone of direct experience of others is the zone of 'mere contemporaries', others who coexist with me in time but whom I do not experience immediately. Thus this kind of knowledge is always indirect and impersonal; it is anonymous. However there are degrees of anonymity within the zone of contemporaries and, indeed, in practice it may often be difficult to distinguish the zone of direct experience (or consociates) from the zone of contemporaries. It may be better therefore to see these two zones as ranged upon a continuum of vividness and anonymity, ranging from direct experience, through the least anonymous regions of contemporaries, that is those that I once encountered face-to-face and whom I could so encounter again, to functionaries such as postmen, and finally to 'objective configurations of meaning' such as the rules of French grammar. Of course I do have knowledge not only of persons, things, or events, that coexist with me in time. I also have knowledge of predecessors and successors. This knowledge will be relatively anonymous like that of contemporaries, but it will also be a good deal more vague, for the social environment of predecessors and successors is quite different from that of contemporaries. I can be pretty sure that the experiences of a contemporary, however remote, will be much like my own, but I cannot depend on such shared experience for interpretation of predecessors; all I have to go on is 'The characteristics of human experience *in general*.' This uncertainty is even more pronounced for successors, for there is no way of discovering what civilization will inform their life-world.

In sum, knowledge of consociates always has the quality of 'existing within a subjective context of meaning, as being the unique experiences of a particular person'.[14] Contemporaries are apprehended as anonymous processes; knowledge of contemporaries is *abstracted* from individual settings. As Schutz says: 'My knowledge of my contemporaries is, therefore, inferential and discursive. It stands, by its essential nature, in an *objective* context of meaning and only in such.'[15]

For Schutz, the abstract quality of the knowledge of contemporaries is very important for it represents a very basic characteristic of the great bulk of our knowledge of the life-world. Thus, knowledge of contemporaries is essentially and necessarily *typified*; it refers not to the individual qualities of persons or things but to their typical qualities, a feature that makes this kind of knowledge usable again and again in different situations.

Generally, objects and persons encountered in everyday life are seen as examples of a type and it is this that makes possible our relationship with them.

> The factual world of our experience . . . is experienced from the outset as a typical one. Objects are experienced as trees, animals, and the like, and more specifically as oaks, firs, maples, or rattlesnakes, sparrows, dogs. . . . What is newly experienced is already known in the sense that it recalls similar or equal things formerly perceived.[16]

The process of typification is best illustrated by consideration of one of the regions of the zone of contemporaries, that of functionaries, persons whose existence is relevant to me only in that they perform certain functions. Thus when I post a letter, I am not interested in the personal characteristics of the postman, but only in those features that make him a typical postman. I do not expect that my letter will be singled out for special treatment, but only that it will be handled in the way that letters typically are.

Not all our knowledge of the world is typified. As I have already indicated, knowledge in the zone of direct experience is not knowledge of types but is knowledge of individual, unique characteristics. From the earlier discussion, one can say that, as knowledge of the world becomes more anonymous as one moves from the zone of direct experience to the zone of contemporaries, so also does the knowledge become more typified.

Relevance and Interest

We are not equally interested in all provinces of the everyday life-world. Some of it is more relevant to us than others. Schutz distinguishes four 'zones of relevance'. Firstly, there is that part of the world directly within our reach which can be dominated, or partially dominated, by us. Knowledge for this zone must be precise and exhaustive. Secondly, there are fields not open to our domination but relevant because they may furnish means to the end of mastering the situation. It is sufficient to have inexact knowledge here, merely of the 'possibilities, the chances, the risks'.

Thirdly, there are zones which, for the moment, have no connection with mastery of the situation. This zone we take for granted. Fourthly, there is a sector of the world that is completely irrelevant. Schutz rather mysteriously says that it is sufficient merely to have 'blind belief in the That and How of things within this zone'.[17]

The Schutzian notion of relevance carries with it the important consideration that our knowledge of the life-world is *selective*. We select knowledge and organize it in zones of decreasing relevance. The earlier discussion of typification raises a similar point. Generally, our knowledge is typified, but we have to select those items in a set of individuals that are relevant for the construction of a type. In other words, the world does not appear to us as an undifferentiated welter of experiences and our knowledge of it is not a random collection of bits of information or belief. We inhabit an *interpreted* world: 'All facts are from the outset, facts selected from a universal context by the activities of our mind. They are therefore always interpreted facts. . . .'[18]

I have said that Schutz considers that the everyday life-world is the paramount reality. However, in living in the everyday world, our attitude is not theoretical or contemplative but *active*. For Schutz, everyday life is a process of dominating, or attempting to dominate, a world that resists us; we have repetitively to master situations and cope with problems. We then acquire that knowledge of the world that is required to further our plans and projects. Or, to use a more familiar notion, also used by Schutz, it is our *interests* that organize our knowledge, form our zones of relevance, and dictate typifications. 'It is our interest at hand that motivates all our thinking, projecting, acting, and therewith establishes the problems to be solved by our thought, and the goals to be attained by our actions. In other words, it is our interest that breaks asunder the unproblematic field of the preknown into various zones of various relevance with respect to such interest.'[19]

In the Introduction I argued that the concept of interest is also important to Marxist sociology of belief. Schutz does not refer to any notion of *this* kind in his own work, but there are those who see significant parallels between the two uses of the concept. Heeren,[20] for example, believes that all exercises in the sociology of knowledge are concerned with the relation between interests 'broadly conceived' and mental products. It is true that there are superficial similarities. Schutz, for example, is very keen to avoid a too psychologistic interpretation of his notion of interest by insisting that there is no such thing as an isolated interest. On the contrary, interests are organized into systems, although these systems are changeable and interests within them may be contradictory. One might attempt to equate a system of interest with a class-interest.

However the Marxist and Schutzian notions of interest are drawn from entirely different conceptual frameworks and there would probably be no point in trying to reconcile them. One way of investigating Schutz's conception further is to ask what is his view of the relationship of social structure and individual autonomy.

Structure and Autonomy

One view of Schutz is that he opposed orthodox sociology and more or less did away with the concept of social structure and substituted the notion of the actor choosing between projects and able to act in a quite unconstrained way. The suggestion is that he was a 'subjectivist' in opposition to the 'objectivist' orthodoxy, and that he made sociological analysis an analysis of consciousness. This view is quite wrong. Although in his earlier work, Schutz develops his theory of action and account of the life-world without explicit repeated reference to a concept of structure, he does not mean to exclude it; rather it is placed 'in brackets'. Further there are hints of his view of the relationship of individual and structure and these receive a more explicit statement in the later *Structures of the Life-World*. [21]

The everyday life-world is not private but is intersubjective, constituted by relations between people who share a common experience of reality.

> We stated before that the world of daily life into which we are born is from the outset an intersubjective world. This implies on the one hand that this world is not my private one but common to all of us; on the other hand that within this world there exist fellow-men with whom I am connected by manifold social relationships. [22]

Thus the knowledge of the life-world is at least partly determined by the necessity of social interaction with others, or, as Schutz says, the stock of knowledge is 'socialized'. That is, the relevance system of each adult 'shows extensive, typical similarities with the subjective relevance systems of fellowmen and contemporaries'. [23]

The importance of the socialization of the subjective stock of knowledge is clearly seen if one considers the way that a child learns. The child is faced by others who all the time insist that he behave in certain ways, or, at the least, that he acts reciprocally. From his very earliest days, the intersubjectivity of the everyday life-world is built into the child's perceptions of the life-world by the actions of those around him. Further, others have socially determined ways of behaving towards him: '. . . with respect to the child they conduct themselves in ways which are determined by social institutions (marriage, fatherhood, etc.) and the child is apprehended by them in socially derived typical forms (such as first-born, son, blessing of God, crutch, etc.).' [24] One of the most important mechanisms in the socialization of the stock of knowledge, is language. Language is by definition an intersubjective medium and provides a way of making subjective experience into an objective social reality. For Schutz, language is a 'given' that everybody has to learn and the very *use* of language is a demonstration of the social determination of knowledge.

In sum, a large part of the stock of knowledge that an individual has at hand is socially determined, even institutionally determined. Thus Schutz frequently refers to the way in which we inhabit a world that is *pre-given*, at least partly by the fact that it is intersubjective. There is also another source of determination outside the individual, for Schutz believes that the particular situation facing the individual also acts as a constraint. However, situational determination and social determination are not the only forces acting on the stock of knowledge, for the unique biography of the individual is also relevant. Thus an individual's knowledge of the everyday life-world is partly socially determined, and partly uniquely constructed by him.

Thus, Schutz is certainly not a 'subjectivist' holding to the view that the individual consciousness is autonomous of social forces. If anything, despite his phenomenological interests, he has a fairly strong notion of the *social* determination of knowledge. To some extent, Schutz's method of working may have contributed to the fairly widespread view that he was a subjectivist. He makes it plain that his method of analysis is to start with the way that individual, subjective experience is constituted, leaving the degree of determination of this knowledge by social institutions 'in brackets', as something assumed but not discussed.

Schutz's view of the relationship of the individual consciousness to social structure has led to criticism from those who would prefer that he had stuck to 'purer' phenomenological principles. Popkin, for example, argues that Schutz has failed 'to be faithful to his fundamental assumption than an analysis of social life must be grounded in the data of human experience, the lived world. Schutz's desire for a synthesis may have caused him to violate the fundamental assumption of his system.'[25] For Popkin, Schutz's attempt to ally phenomenology with some conception of social science, necessarily means the sacrifice of phenomenology, for scientific categories, as employed by Schutz, are categories of social structure that are not used by actors in the everyday world. A similar argument is advanced by Gorman, although from a different perspective, in that he appears to prefer the science to the phenomenology. Gorman argues that Schutz is faced by two divergent alternatives. Either actors freely choose, uninfluenced by social structures. 'Alternatively, if socially derived typifications do determine our behaviour, then there is little more than hypocrisy in contending we are free, self-determining, meaning-endowing actors. Our behaviour, in this case is the determined result of variables existing independent of us. . . .'[26] In Gorman's view, Schutz does not choose between these two possibilities, but adopts the totally implausible position that actors 'freely' perform actions, and hold knowledge, that they would exhibit were their behaviour determined by social structure.

There is, therefore, a certain tension within Schutz's position which he does not satisfactorily resolve explicitly, although, as I have argued, he tended, especially in his later work, to stress social determinations. In addition, one should beware of the conservatism, noted earlier, of his characterization of the life-world as an unquestioned reality. There seems no real reason to hold such a view, especially given that individuals are seen as creative and meaning-endowing. It seems equally plausible to see the everyday world as contradictory and incoherent, and individuals' relationships to it as being constituted by doubt and frustration, rather than the *suspension* of doubt. This conservatism is clearly closely related to the neglect of issues that are central to the Marxist analysis of consciousness. Thus, Schutz seems relatively uninterested in such problems as power and the unequal distribution of knowledge, or the relationship of knowledge to the allocation of individuals to particular places in society.[27]

---

8 BERGER AND LUCKMANN

I have presented Schutz as answering, among other things, questions about the relationship of structure and individual autonomy. In a way this is a rather artificial method of presentation since Schutz would not have recognized this as a central problem. As a phenomenological philosopher, he was interested mainly in the constitution of the life-world, and although one can extract from his writings particular views about social structure or institutions, to do so is to impose a characteristically sociological set of concerns on to his work.

Berger and Luckmann have a great and acknowledged debt to Schutz. The net effect of the incorporation of his work into theirs is to sociologize Schutz, to bring his concerns into an orthodox sociological framework. If Schutz's principal interest is in the life-world, Berger and Luckmann's, at least in their book *The Social Construction of Reality*, is in the relationship of individual and social structure. They dislike current sociological conceptions of this relationship because they tend to be deterministic, seeing the individual as moulded by social structure.

A reformulation of the relationship of individual and structure, as it applies in the sociology of knowledge, is the object of *The Social Construction of Reality*. My method in this chapter will be to examine this book in some detail, drawing in other work by the two authors where it is relevant to the analysis of the sociology of knowledge. Both Berger and Luckmann have published voluminously,[1] both together and separately, mainly in the sociology of religion. However they regard the sociology of knowledge as a central, if not *the* central, theoretical discipline within sociology, and *The Social Construction of Reality* is thus an important text within their work as a whole.

Knowledge in Everyday Life

Berger and Luckmann believe that one of the main weaknesses of analyses in the sociology of knowledge, besides their determinism, is their concentration on *theoretical thought* or, worse, on the written ideas of intellectuals. Instead the sociology of knowledge should analyse 'everything that passes for Knowledge in society'.[2] Within knowledge defined in this way, theoretical speculation plays only a minor role. What is of much greater importance is the knowledge appropriate to the conduct of everyday life and, following Schutz, Berger and Luckmann believe that the reality of everyday life is the *paramount* reality.

Their starting point is therefore a phenomenological description (refraining 'from any causal or genetic hypotheses') of the knowledge appropriate to the everyday world, a description that more or less reproduces Schutz's discussion of the same subject.

The everyday life-world is experienced as an ordered reality, an intersubjective reality, shared with others, and also an objective reality—that is, a reality 'out there' which appears independent of my volition. However it only *appears* to be independent of my volition and the process by which human creativity becomes objectified plays an important role in Berger and Luckmann's analysis. Indeed social life is possible only by means of such objectivations, because it is only in this way that I can become aware of the subjective motives, intentions and feelings of others. For example, I have an argument with a man who throws a knife at me while I am in bed asleep. In the morning I wake up with the knife embedded in the wall above my bed.

> The knife qua object expresses my adversary's anger. It affords me access to his subjectivity. . . . Indeed, if I leave the object where it is, I can look at it again the following morning and . . . other men can come and look it it. In other words, the knife in my wall has become an objectively available constituent of the reality I share with my adversary and with other men.[3]

The knife is acting as a sign, and signs are a crucial case of objectivation. In turn, language is the most important system of signs. It is language that maintains the common objectivations of everyday life. It can transcend the face-to-face situation; it typifies and anonymizes. Language enables the construction of a common stock of knowledge and its transmission.

The knowledge of everyday life is organized in zones around my 'here-and-now'. The centre of my social world is myself. Around this centre, knowledge is arranged in zones, both spatial and temporal, of decreasing relevance. Spatially, the nearest zone is that directly accessible to bodily manipulation while, temporally, the nearest zone is that of elements of the world contemporary with me.

Experience of others is also arranged in zones radiating outwards from myself. Nearest and most important is the face-to-face situation, regarded by Berger and Luckmann as prototypical. Knowledge of others experienced in this way is direct and 'vivid'. They are persons whose qualities are unique. However, much of our knowledge of others is not acquired in face-to-face encounters. This kind of knowledge is typified; we select out those characteristics that interest us and ignore those that may make these persons unique. For example, we are not generally interested in the qualities of the postman other than those typical qualities that make him a postman. Thus, zones of knowledge moving away from direct face-to-face encounters are more typified and more anonymous. Similar points can be made about our experiences of others who are not our contemporaries. Since we cannot have face-to-face relationships with predecessors or successors, our knowledge of them is bound to be typified.

Everyday life is dominated by the pragmatic motive, that is everyday life is essentially oriented to solving practical problems. Given the importance of this motive, recipe knowledge, that is 'knowledge limited to pragmatic competence in routine performances', occupies a prominent place in the stock of knowledge. For example, one builds up a stock of recipe knowledge about how to use the telephone and this includes knowledge of how to get it repaired. The validity of this type of knowledge is pragmatically taken for granted until it comes across a problem which cannot be solved.

Berger and Luckmann adopt Schutz's view of the way that interests structure the stock of knowledge via a system of relevances. Perhaps they emphasize the intersubjective character of everyday life even more than Schutz, for they stress the way in which relevance structures can be determined by 'My general situation in society' as well as by immediate pragmatic motives. Further, relevance structures intersect, so that an important element of knowledge of the external world is the relevance structures of others.

Having described the structure of the stock of knowledge, Berger and Luckmann's next problem is to show how it is constructed and maintained. They insist that the process of construction is essentially dialectical—a dialectic of subject and object, of individual and society.

The Dialectical Method

Berger and Luckmann's method appears to be very eclectic in its origins. Their anthropological presuppositions are strongly influenced by Marx and their social psychology is drawn from Mead. Their view of the nature of social reality depends a good deal on Durkheim, although his views are modified by the development of a dialectical principle derived from Marx which incorporates an emphasis on the construction of social reality through subjective meanings derived from Weber. The dialectical method can be illustrated by showing how it integrates propositions central to the writings of both Durkheim and Weber, two theorists whose work is often thought to be irreconcilable. Durkheim says, 'Consider social facts as things', while Weber observes, 'The object of cognigion is the subjective meaning complex of action.' Durkheim seems to argue for a position in which individuals are moulded by social structure while Weber appears to believe that analysis has to start with subjective meaning. However, 'these two statements are not contradictory. Society does indeed possess objective facticity. And society is indeed built up by activity that expresses subjective meaning.'[4] For society has a dual character of both objective facticity and subjective meaning. It is a dialectical process in which subjective meanings become objective facticities and objective facticities become subjective meanings. It has to say something about the way in which objective structures of knowledge are ceated by individual consciousness and how individual con- sciousness acquires objective knowledge.

The dialectic has three 'moments', externalization, objectivation and internalization. The following extract from Berger's *The Social Reality of Religion* gives a good account of these:

> Externalization is the ongoing outpouring of human being into the world, both in the physical and the mental activity of men. Objectivation is the attainment of the products of this activity (again both physical and mental) of a reality that confronts its original producers as a facticity external to, and other than, themselves. Internalization is the reappropriation by men of this same reality, transforming it once again from structures of the objective world into structures of the subjective consciousness. It is through externalization that society is a human product. It is through objectivation that society becomes a reality sui genesis. It is through internalization that man is a product of society.[5]

I have already said that the dialectical approach is seen as an alternative to a determinism in which the individual is formed by social structure. Berger and Luckmann believe that determinist theories reify social reality by denying that there is a sense in which individuals create the social world around them. Such theories see the social world as rather like the physical world, that is, as composed of thing-like elements which impose themselves on people. However reification is not only a theoretical matter for it is also a feature of the knowledge of everyday life. That is, because the social world appears to men as such a massive, real and coercive fact, they tend to invest it with thing-like qualities, as being a reality that presses down on them. The reification of everyday perception of social reality is an instance of a larger process, that of alienation, which is again very general to social life. For Berger and Luck- mann, men are alienated when they forget that the social reality which appears to be so massive is in fact a human creation, is *their* creation.

Society as Objective Reality

Having described the structure of our knowledge of the external world, Berger and Luckmann's method of exposition is to show the workings of the dialectic in the constitution, firstly, of objective reality, and then of subjective reality.

Before considering their account of the construction of objective reality, it is necessary to explore a set of fundamental assumptions made by Berger and Luckmann, for their work as a whole is explicitly based on a kind of philosophical anthropology.

'Man occupies a peculiar position in the animal kingdom.'[6] Generally, animals have a fixed relationship to their environment. That is, each animal species has an environment which is specific to it. For example there are 'dog-worlds' and 'horse-worlds'. 'In this sense, all non-human animals, as species and as individuals, live in closed worlds whose structures are predetermined by the biological equipment of the several animal species.'[7] This is not true of man, whose biological equipment does not specially fit him for a particular environment. There is no 'man-world'. The 'world-openness' of man's relationship with his environment derives from several connected factors. The fundamental point is that man's instinctual structure is relatively unspecialized compared with that of animals. In addition, the human child is at birth very much less biologically developed than most other comparable mammals. The result is that, in man, a good deal of what might otherwise be 'biologically' determined development takes place in active interaction with the environment, social as well as physical. Man is thus born with a relatively plastic nature which is then formed, to a great extent, by the social and cultural environment. Although of course, there are biological constraints on the human condition, it is in this sense that one can say that man is a social creature in a way that animals are not.

However the same biological factors which make human nature plastic and hence uniquely social, also make it unstable. The unformed human being cannot cope with its environment; it has to be moulded by social forces. Social order transforms a biologically given world-openness into a socially given world-closedness. Thus, for Berger and Luckmann, the process of transformation from a plastic to a formed nature is simultaneously a process of ordering.

There is, however, a curious gap in their argument at this point, which is symptomatic of their whole approach. They argue, conventionally perhaps, that human beings are less formed at birth than are animals and are less able to cope with their environment. They move from this claim to saying that human nature is, at birth, unstable, and that the most important requirement of the process of socialization is the construction of *order*. One might have thought that socialization involves all sorts of other things, including the provision of certain sorts of skills necessary for coping with the physical environment, and that this provision is fundamentally important. If there was no process of socialization, and a human being had to rely on the skills available at birth, it would simply die. However Berger and Luckmann seem to think that without socialization, human existence would be merely *chaos*. 'Human existence, if it were thrown back on its organismic resources by themselves, would be existence in some sort of chaos.'[8] 'Chaos' is an odd way to describe such an extreme contingency. It is nonetheless revealing, for Berger and Luckmann are deriving *order* as the prime requirement of human existence from the incompleteness of the human being at birth. Not only is it eccentric to suggest that order is *fundamental* in this sense, Berger and Luckmann do not succeed in showing how *order* is derived from the biological facts of human infancy. At times they attempt to derive order from other postulates. For example, in *The Social Reality of Religion*, Berger says, 'Put differently, the most important function of society is nomization. The anthropological presupposition for this is a human craving for meaning that appears to have the force of instinct. Men are congenitally compelled to impose a meaningful order upon reality.'[9] This is not exactly an attempt to derive order from human nature, it is a suggestion that order *is* human nature.

Berger and Luckmann make clear that these biological facts do not imply any *particular* social order, they merely imply the fundamental necessity of social order in general. Further, it is not the case that order is biologically constructed. Although it is, in a sense, biologically *required*, social order is constructed *socially*. Put differently, externalization, the process by which men seek to construct their social order, is rooted in the human biological constitution, although it is a social process and its form is socially determined. It is an 'anthropological necessity'. In order to understand how social order is constructed, maintained and transmitted, apart from these anthropological necessities, one must have a theory of institutionalization.

The process of institutionalization begins with the patterned, habitual, repetition of human action. Again, this is seen as a constant of human behaviour; generally human action is repeated in much the same form. Social institutions, in that they are patterned sequences of action, result from habitualization. However the crucial feature of institutions is that they involve the interlocking of the habitualized actions of a variety of actors. 'Institutionalization occurs whenever there is a reciprocal typification of habitualized actions by types of actors.'[10] Institutions, therefore, are shared typifications; the institution posits that particular typical actions are performed by particular typical actors.

One can illustrate the way that an institution is built up by considering the way that two actors, A and B, coming from entirely different social worlds, interact. In this interaction, typifications will be produced quickly. As A watches B act and then sees these actions recur, he is able to construct these actions as typical and can posit typical motives from them. A will also assume that B is doing the same thing with regard to him. Eventually A and B will begin to play roles with respect to each other and will make each other's roles act as models for their own role-playing. 'For example, B's role in the activity of preparing food is not only typified as such by A, but enters as a constitutive element into A's own food-preparation role. Thus a collection of reciprocally typified actions will emerge, habitualized for each in roles, some of which will be performed separately some in common.'[11] As A and B interact, as a set of reciprocal typifications are evolved, a routine is developed, in which actions that originally caused surprise, become trivial and taken-for-granted. A measure of routine provides a background against which it is possible for A and B to innovate in their behaviour towards each other. These innovations become habitualized, further expanding the background common to A and B. 'In other words, a social world will be in process of construction, containing within it the roots of an expanding institutional order.'[12]

Institutionalization, however, perfects itself only when it is passed on to others, when, for example, A and B have children. When just A and B are involved, their social world has a tenuous quality. As they made it so they can unmake it. This is not true of their children, for they are born into a world which they did not make. To them the social world is a massive fact experienced as possessing a reality of its own. It is, in other words, an *objective* fact. Berger and Luckmann emphasize the manner in which the social world does confront individuals.

> The institutions, as historical and objective facticities, confront the individual as undeniable facts. The institutions are *there*, external to him, persistent in their reality, whether he likes them or not. He cannot wish them away. They resist his attempts to change or evade them. They have coercive power over him, both in themselves, by the sheer force of their facticity, and through the control mechanisms that are usually attached to the most important of them.[13]

The story of A and B provides an illustration of the formation and transmission of institutions and also of two moments of the dialectic. Firstly, we are shown how A and B *externalize* in creating the institution and then we see how these externalizations become objectivated when it becomes a question of involving others in the institution created by A and B. However the institutional order of a society is not a seamless web, uniformly and successfully massive. There are a number of ways in which it may be imperfectly formed, or imperfectly objectivated. Institutions become objective facticities when they are passed on from generation to generation. The new generation does not know the rationale and meaning of the institution. To them, therefore, institutions may be objective but they are also unexplained. Further there is no *a priori* reason to suppose that different institutional processes are well integrated with one another. Since each institution will have a different history there is likely to be some segmentation of institutions. This implies a potential for discord, not only between participants in different institutional processes, but also within one individual as he is involved in different institutions. These imperfections demand some mechanism of reconciliation. Such a mechanism is also required by a much more general characteristic of the social world than institutional imperfection, for Berger and Luckmann believe that the world is endemically, fundamentally and systematically chaotic. On this subject they can be lyrical: 'The thought keeps suggesting itself. . . . That, perhaps, the bright reality of everyday life is but an illusion, to be swallowed up at any moment by the howling nightmares of the other, the night-side of reality.'[14] Again, '*All* social reality is precarious. All societies are constructions in the face of chaos.'[15] However, as we have already seen, social order is an anthropological necessity. Thus, there must be procedures which restore or maintain order in an intrinsically chaotic social world. These procedures are generically known, perhaps rather unfortunately, as legitimations. The notion that the world is fundamentally chaotic is an abiding theme in the work of Berger and Luckmann and one should note that, yet again, their argument is based on some assumed *constant* of social reality, in this case, the precariousness of the world.

Legitimations, then throw some kind of protective canopy over fragile social reality, in such a way that people have their lives meaningfully ordered; they put everything in its right place. Four levels of legitimation can be distinguished, differentiated by the degree to which they are theoretical. Firstly, language itself is legitimating, for legitimating explanations are built into the vocabulary. Thus the fact of naming another person a cousin, legitimates the behaviour that is appropriate to cousinhood. (It should be remembered that the term 'legitimation' is being used in a much wider sense than, say, 'justify'.) The second level of legitimation is made up of proverbs, maxims and folk tales which provide a slightly more theoretical way of making everyday events meaningful. Thirdly, there are more or less explicit theories about particular institutional sectors, theories which may make up a differentiated body of knowledge, administered by specialists. For example, a theory of the rights and duties of cousinhood might be developed and promulgated by the old men of the tribe. 'Symbolic universes' make up the fourth level of legitimation. These are theories that integrate all institutional processes, that provide a total and overarching system of meaning. All events can be given a meaning within a symbolic universe which can have this totally encompassing character, precisely because they are symbolic; that is, they refer to realities which do not occur in everyday experience.

They are also theoretical, although it is, of course, possible to inhabit a symbolic universe untheoretically, as, for Berger and Luckmann, most people do. However the importance of symbolic universes, and their total and theoretical character, means that they tend to be promulgated by experts, who will also specialize in a kind of second-order activity by legitimating the symbolic universes. In the case of religions, for example, there are always theologians or priests who strive to present the religion as a coherent body of meaning.

It is uncertain from their works which level of legitimation Berger and Luckmann believe to be the most significant. In *The Social Reality of Religion*, Berger believes the pre-theoretical level to be the most important, perhaps because it is so pervasive. In *The Social Construction of Reality*, however, symbolic universes are given more emphasis. At any event, it is plain that legitimating agencies cover a very wide range. One of the most important of such agencies is religion, a topic on which both Berger and Luckmann have written a good deal. The legitimating role of religion is, incidentally, one of the main reasons for the intimate connection between the sociology of knowledge and the sociology of religion in the work of Berger and Luckmann.

Religion is, historically, the most obviously successful symbolic universe. In that its symbolism is typically far removed from the realities of everyday experience, it is able to provide a peculiarly all-embracing framework of legitimation. It is able to provide individuals with a means of coping with 'marginal situations', particularly death, which are otherwise deeply threatening. It can achieve the integration of all discrete institutional processes so that 'the entire society now makes sense'. In the past, 'religion' meant formal church religion but, more recently, there has been a decline of these public religious observances. Berger and Luckmann suggest that church religion has been replaced by other agencies, not only a more private religious commitment, but also by such systems of belief as psychiatry or communism.[16] Indeed Luckmann comes close, not only to equating religion with substitutes for it such as psychiatry, but also to equating it with the process of legitimation itself. A sociology of legitimation is thus effectively a sociology of religion. 'We may conclude, therefore, that the world view, as an 'objective' and historical social reality, performs an essentially religious function and define it as an elementary social form of religion. This social form is universal in society.'[17] It should be said that Berger deliberately avoids such a reductionist conclusion.

Religion is an effective agency of legitimation because it creates an ordered and total world in which all experience has a meaningful place. Religion makes the world seem an objective fact independent of man's volition. However, the more effective it is in this function, the more alienating a force it becomes, for plainly the more autonomous and coercive a religiously legitimated world is, the more man is unable to conceive of his role in creating and maintaining that world.[18] Thus religion is a powerful force for reification. For example, instead of perceiving marriage as a socially constructed institution, it may be reified as a mere imitation of divine acts of creation. Of course, it is not only religion that alienates and reifies as it legitimates. Any legitimation agent, in that it provides a total and objective canopy of meaning, will do the same.

I have been arguing that one of the most central and determining images in the work of Berger and Luckmann is that social life is systematically disordered and *fundamentally* chaotic and that these terrors are kept at bay only by a canopy of legitimations. There is something wrong with the question, 'Is social life fundamentally chaotic or ordered?' and this is especially so as Berger and Luckmann nominate so many candidates as legitimation agencies. For example Berger says that 'all socially objectivated "knowledge" is legitimating'.[19] Legitimation becomes such a general category that it is almost as if social life was required to keep social life ordered. Further, the agencies of legitimation seem so successful that the *normal* condition of life is order. Given these points, one might ask what is the value or validity of a philosophical anthropology that insisted that disorder was fundamentally constitutive of social reality. Indeed as I argued earlier, it is by no means clear that Berger and Luckmann successfully demonstrate the precariousness of social reality, at least in as much as they try to derive it from the plasticity of human nature at birth. There are other connected difficulties with Berger and Luckmann's position. Firstly it could be argued that man can tolerate a good deal of uncertainty, without the need of a legitimating apparatus, and of course it has been suggested that the human condition positively benefits from a measure of risk and uncertainty. Doubtless human nature requires a certain minimum of stability, but that does not tell one how much is required. That is, it is possible that Berger and Luckmann *at best* establish the anthropological necessity of *some* order, but move from this to exaggerate the amount of order demanded. A similar argument is advanced by Light.[20] He suggests that Berger and Luckmann have a demonic view of social uncertainty often described in imagery which appears to be religiously inspired. States of uncertainty are fatal to the human condition. In Light's view Berger and Luckmann are therefore obsessed with the necessity of certainty and they believe that the basic mode of human cognition is the drive for certainty. However such a concentration neglects those processes that systematically create *uncertainty* and the independent importance of uncertainty itself. Berger and Luckmann see the significance of periods of mass uncertainty only in terms of the way that they lead up to periods of certainty. Why should it not be the other way round? Certainty is important only because it contrasts with uncertainty which is the true basis of human nature. Light concedes that social stability may be important but not as important as social survival and, for the latter, uncertainty may be as functional as certainty.

A second difficulty in Berger and Luckmann's position concerns an ambiguity in the conception of social stability. Sometimes they talk of legitimation as giving *meaning* and sometimes as giving *order* or *certainty*. However these are very different notions and will not always run together. It is possible for a system of belief to give meaning but create uncertainty. To some extent this point is realized in *The Social Construction of Reality* where a distinction is made between cognitive and normative aspects of legitimating systems. Thus there is a difference between saying that 'X is your sister' and saying that people should not sleep with their sisters. Nonetheless, Berger and Luckmann do not realize that there may be a certain tension between giving meaning in the sense of explaining and giving order in the sense of moral certainty; one can give meaning without giving certainty.

Society as Subjective Reality

The dialectic of externalization, objectivation and internalization now has to be applied to subjective reality. For objective reality there is not a sequence of these three moments, but for the individual's biography there is. The process begins with internalization which is 'the immediate apprehension or interpretation of an objective event, as expressing meaning, that is, as a manifestation of another's subjective processes which thereby become meaningful to myself'.[21] More generally, internalization is an understanding of one's fellowmen and the apprehension of the world as a meaningful reality. Berger and Luckmann's treatment of internalization is essentially a discussion of the traditional problem of socialization although it is presented in a fairly unconventional way.

There is firstly a distinction between primary and secondary socialization. Primary socialization is effectively childhood socialization by which the individual becomes a member of society. Secondary socialization is any subsequent process that inducts an individual into a new sector of social life.

Berger and Luckmann's discussion of primary socialization is heavily dependent on the social psychology of Mead. Every individual is born into a social structure; there is a fixed objective world there before his arrival. He encounters the 'significant others'—parents, siblings and so on—who have responsibility for his socialization. The definitions of reality provided by the significant others will appear to the child as objective facts over which he has no control. The child identifies with the significant others, that is he takes on their roles and internalizes them. By being able to take on the role of others, the child is able to see himself through their eyes. Thus the process of taking on another's role is also a process of self-identification. The self is therefore a reflected identity. Socialization proceeds from taking on the role of significant others to a more general identification. This process is founded on the realization by the child that the attitudes and roles of his significant others are, in fact, more widely shared. Instead of taking on the role of significant others only, the child is able to take on the role of the 'generalized other'. He now has an identity, not only *vis-à-vis* particular persons, but an identity in general. This is a decisive phase for 'it implies the internalization of society as such and of the objective reality established therein, and, at the same time, the subjective establishment of a coherent and continuous identity. Society, identity, and reality are subjectively crystallized in the same process of internalization.'[22]

The child undergoing a process of socialization has to accept his significant others. Consequently, the world presented by the significant others is not internalized as one world among many possible, but as *the* world. This is why primary socializations are generally more firmly entrenched than secondary socializations can be.

The necessity of secondary socialization arises in any society in which there is a considerable division of labour, and hence some differentiation of institutional processes. Secondary socialization is then the internalization of particular institutional processes. As I have already indicated, secondary socializations are not nearly so well entrenched as primary ones. It is no longer a question of internalizing *the* world but of internalizing sub-worlds. Further, those involved in the transmission of institutional realities are not so much 'significant others' as functionaries with whom there is little emotional involvement. All these points indicate the fairly obvious conclusion that secondary socialization is of less social significance than primary socialization.

So far, I have presented socialization as an efficient method of induction into social reality. This is far from being the case for Berger and Luckmann, for there are a number of imperfections that are systematic to the whole process. Thus socialization can never, in the nature of things, be complete. Again, since secondary socialization must build on primary socialization, there is always the possibility of inconsistency between the two. Further, with any degree of social differentiation, the actual content of the socialization process will differ as between different social groups. In most societies therefore, there will be competing definitions of reality which may well be threatening to individuals. These imperfections indicate that socialization cannot ever be totally successful in the sense that there will always be a lack of fit between subjective reality and objective reality.[23] That is, the reality that is subjectively appropriated, which results from socialization, cannot ever quite match objective reality. In Berger's view, this lack of fit produces a division of consciousness, into socialized and non-socialized components, which 'results in an internal confrontation between socialized and non-socialized components of self, reiterating within consciousness itself the external confrontation between society and the individual'.[24]

The lack of success of socialization means that 'every viable society must develop procedures of reality-maintenance to safeguard a measure of symmetry between objective and subjective reality'.[25] This is the same problem as that already discussed in connection with legitimation. Now the emphasis is on the protection of subjective reality rather than objective, institutionally defined, reality. In a similar manner, Berger and Luckmann suggest that reality-maintaining procedures are also demanded, separately from the imperfections of socialization, by the innate instability of everyday life. Everyday life may seem solid and real enough, but 'it is threatened by the marginal situations of human experience. . . . There is always the haunting presence of metamorphoses, those actually remembered and those only sensed as sinister possibilities.'[26] These marginal situations represent the subjective side of the precariousness of all socially constructed worlds discussed at some length earlier in this chapter, and the marginal situation *par excellence* is death. Death threatens the taken-for-granted realities more than anything else and its incorporation within some meaningful structure is of paramount importance.

The most effective device which maintains reality against ever present terror is the simple routine of everyday interaction with others. The continuation of everyday life, as it has always been, confirms my identity as an everyday person. In effect, subjective reality is maintained in the same way as it was created and by similar personnel. Thus, it is the set of significant others who, in their daily interactions, are chiefly responsible for repetitively confirming the individual's identity, supported by a chorus of less significant others. However, there is an important sense in which everybody is involved in reality-maintenance, simply by continuing to behave in a 'normal', routine way.

If it is daily life that generally maintains reality, it is conversation that specifically sustains it. It is not that conversation is always about the meaning of life, but rather that every conversational exchange necessarily presupposes a whole world, a whole background of shared assumptions which are implictly invoked and confirmed by every sentence spoken. An experiment conducted by Garfinkel nicely illustrates this point.[27] He asked a married couple to write down an ordinary conversation that they had had one morning. It quickly became apparent that the conversation made sense only to the participants because they shared a set of background assumptions which effectively filled out the more telegraphic spoken words. He then asked them to write down those background assumptions that they thought made sense of their interchange. The couple found that this was almost impossible because every assumption that they recorded was in turn dependent on further assumptions, and so on. The efficacy of conversation in the maintenance of reality depends on the objectifying power of language. In the discussion of objective reality I indicated how important language was to Berger and Luckmann in the creation of an ordered, objective world. In conversation, the objectifications of language became part of the individual consciousness. Thus, in a very basic sense, everyone who employs language is maintaining reality.

In sum, subjective reality is maintained principally by everyday life. Berger and Luckmann suggest that the force of this claim can best be appreciated by considering what happens when everyday routines are disrupted. Thus, odd, random, or unexplained, behaviour on the part of others, particularly significant others, can have shattering consequences for the individual; he may literally not know who he is. Indeed this point is the basis of certain kinds of film. Hitchcock, for example, is a director who makes a good deal of use of the consequences of the sudden disruption of everyday life, perhaps in the case of mistaken identity. Films of this kind derive their peculiar terror from the feeling that, if others around one start behaving in a quite different way, then one may not be the person one thought one was. Further poignancy is often added by the contrast between the collapse of the everyday world of the central character and the maintenance of the everyday world of others remote from him. Thus the hero, pursued by nameless and inexplicable terrors, may run through a street crowded with shoppers going about their normal occasions. Often his fears are compounded by the fact that his disrupted world is insulated from the normal world. For some reason he cannot have recourse to the normal world of shoppers who might otherwise be sympathetic, and he has to grapple with the new identity that the new, terrifying world is trying to thrust upon him.

The terror that we, as spectators, feel when confronted by such dramatic disruptions often seems quite out of proportion. A similar kind of point is made by yet another of Garfinkel's experiments.[28] In this he persuaded his students to take literally certain entirely conventional conversational gambits. Thus the question, 'How are you?' would be greeted with a minute and exact description of bodily states or with the response, 'What do you mean, How am I?'. In another version, students would go home and try to behave, say, as a lodger, instead of what they were, son, daughter, wife or husband. Plainly the point of these experiments was to see what would happen when everyday reality was experimentally disrupted. In fact the response on the part of those whose routine was thus disturbed was extraordinarily violent, seemingly disproportionately so. This shows the importance of everyday interaction as well as the frightening consequences of its even temporary destruction.

Although socialization is often thought of as a rigid process, the implication of Berger and Luckmann's remarks is that subjective reality can be transformed. In its most drastic form, this will be a total transformation of the kind that occurs in religious conversion. This is in effect a process of resocialization which will involve the destruction of previous socialization, both primary and secondary. The most important requirement for conversion processes of this kind is the existence of a legitimating apparatus not only for the new reality but also for the rejection of the old. Conversion or 'alternation' is only an extreme form of the transformation of subjective reality. In a sense, secondary socialization is also such a transformation. There will be a whole range of resocializations, of varying degrees of thoroughness, between secondary socialization and alternation, and in modern society such processes will be commonplace as individuals are socially and geographically mobile between different social worlds.

It will be obvious from this discussion of subjective reality that the creation and maintenance of identity is closely bound up with the creation and maintenance of subjective reality. Therefore, theoretical work in social psychology is intimately connected with the sociology of knowledge, as it is defined by Berger and Luckmann. A theory of identity *is* a theory of the appropriation of a particular reality.

Conclusions

Despite some of their avowed intentions, the net effect of Berger and Luckmann's work is conservative. The drawbacks of this implicit emphasis emerge in three ways: in the stress on order, in the theoretical use of constants of human nature, and in actual, as opposed to intended, use of their dialectical method.

Berger and Luckmann describe the vices of social disorder in glowing terms; their prose is at its most lyrical and extreme in the passages on this subject.[29] The very seriousness of disorder for the human condition gives order-making devices an enormous importance and necessity. Social certainty is thus a functional requirement prior to any other. This emphasis, however, neglects the creative role of uncertainty and disorder in human affairs; order in other words, is not the only, or the most important, functional imperative.

All of the work of Berger and Luckmann is explicitly based on the assertion of a number of constants of human behaviour—anthropological necessities, like the necessity of externalization which 'apply to any empirically available case of human society'.[30] There is some doubt as to the role of such assumptions in any social theory, in particular, as to how one can establish them. However, as I have tried to argue in this chapter, Berger and Luckmann additionally have some difficulty in deriving their more specific propositions from the anthropological necessities. Furthermore, anthropological necessities are not the only constancies of human nature cited by Berger and Luckmann. Certain biological facts like death, sleep, hunger, sloth and forgetfulness also play an important theoretical role, apart from any merits that they may have as amusing literary diversion from an otherwise fairly straightlaced text. The effect of these points is to suggest that the range of human action is *very* much limited by human nature. In this chapter, I have suggested that Berger and Luckmann set these limits too stringently, which is odd in view of their repeated emphasis on sociality and on the *social* construction of reality.

The dialectical method is of great importance in *The Social Construction of Reality* since Berger and Luckmann are at great pains to correct the mechanical determinism which they believe has characterized most work in the sociology of knowledge. There are a number of passages in their writings which emphasize individual autonomy. Thus Berger says in *The Social Reality of Religion*: 'The individual is not molded as a passive, inert thing. Rather he is formed in the course of a protracted conversation . . . in which he is a participant. . . . Furthermore, once the individual is formed as a person . . . he must continue to participate in the conversation that sustains him as a person in his ongoing biography.'[31] However, despite these avowed intentions, I believe that Berger and Luckmann tend to stress the external constraints rather than the individual autonomy. In discussions of the manner in which society imposes on the individual, they are a great deal more specific, and their phrasing is more extensive and precise. The result is that individual autonomy becomes a residual category, more often asserted than explained. It is suggested, for example, that in socialization individuals take over the world, even if each taking-over is unique. However we are not fully told in what ways it is unique nor whether individual autonomy in this respect is as *important* as social constraint. Doubtless there is some room for individual autonomy, but how much room? The difficulty is most acute when Berger and Luckmann want to say that individuals *ongoingly* modify objective reality. Given their own assertion of the massivity and coerciveness of objective reality, we need to know in some detail what are the sources of this individual creativity.

This general lack of specificity indicates that Berger and Luckmann are much more structurally determinist than they would like to claim. Indeed at times they seem to contradict their own principles: 'The priority of the institutional definitions of situations must be consistently maintained over individual temptations at redefinition.'[32] Robertson puts much the same point in a rather different way: '. . . although the work of Berger and Luckmann starts from the individual and stresses the individual's social and cultural creativity, the nature of the creativity . . . is basically . . . a pessimistic one.'[33]

It is therefore uncertain how deep the phenomenological critique mounted by Berger and Luckmann goes. As far as recasting the *object* of the sociology of knowledge is concerned, they are fairly clear. Analysis must focus on the 'paramount' reality of everyday life. However, in respect of the crucial question of the relation of the individual subject to the structures of social relations, Berger and Luckmann, and Schutz for that matter, are rather less radical than their polemic might indicate.

Conclusion

The Comparison of Theories

In this book, I have been interested in comparing various theories in the sociology of knowledge. Before summarizing some of the main arguments, I want to consider two possible objections to the whole enterprise of theoretical comparison. First, it might be argued that the object of analysis differs as between the three approaches examined; that is, they are literally not talking about the same thing. Thus, the conventional sociology of knowledge looks at categories of knowledge or belief, the critical Marxist perspectives studies ideology, while phenomenological sociology of knowledge takes the 'social construction of reality' as its object. Now, while Berger and Luckmann argue for a sociology of knowledge that goes beyond theoretical formulations to 'what people "know" as "reality" in their everyday, non- or pre-theoretical lives', or to 'common-sense knowledge rather than "ideas"',[1] theirs is effectively a plea for the *extension* of the subject into these areas. They are not proposing a discipline with a completely different object. It might be argued, however, that 'ideology' does denote a concept radically different from 'knowledge', or 'belief'. Now, it is certainly necessary to be careful about the specification of the object of the sociology of knowledge, but there is nothing mysterious about the concept of ideology. None of the concepts, ideology, knowledge, belief, are theory-neutral, but the problem with ideology is that it carries with it a large volume of theoretical baggage, in particular the notion of distortion. A debate between the conventional sociology of knowledge and the theory of ideology is not therefore a debate about the *object* of analysis but a debate about rival social *theories* of knowledge. What appears as an argument about terms or objects of study is, in reality, an argument about theories. Ideology is still a *form* of belief, even if one separately wishes to argue that its social causation has some impact on its validity.[2]

The second objection to comparison of rival sociological theories of knowledge is more basic. Debates within sociology often take the form of debates about fundamental assumptions, epistemologies, or ontologies,[3] rather than about substantive theories. To some extent, this pursuit of fundamental differences between schools or approaches is a peculiar quirk of sociologists and is in need of sociological explanation. More seriously, the *relationship* between sets of epistemological and ontological assumptions and substantive theories supposedly based on them is unclear. An epistemology does not specify what propositions about the social world can be 'derived' from it. Further, there is no reason to suppose that particular theories, even if 'derived' from different assumptions, cannot stand in some meaningful relationship to one another, such that, for example, they can be compared or even integrated. Again, there is no critical theoretical difference between apparently similar propositions formulated within different epistemological/ontological frameworks. For example, Poulantzas has mounted what amounts to an epistemological/ontological attack on theories of ideology like that adopted by Miliband. Nonetheless, it is not clear what difference, if any, this makes to his sociological practice. Thus both Miliband and Poulantzas have not dissimilar positions on the 'dominant ideology'. Poulantzas suggests that '. . . within a social formation ideology is dominated by the ensemble of representations, values, notions, beliefs, etc, by means of which class domination is perpetuated: in other words, it is dominated by what can be called the ideology of the dominant class'.[4] Miliband argues that 'the dominant classes . . . have been able, in conditions of open political competition, to ensure the continuance . . . of economic and political predominance' and 'to foster acceptance of a *capitalist* social order and of its values, an adaptation to its requirements, a rejection of alternatives to it' by a 'process of massive indoctrination'.[5]

I conclude that there is no reason, in principle, to suppose that the three approaches considered in this book are *incomparable* because of their allegedly different epistemological and ontological bases; theories can be compared without such comparison necessarily collapsing into epistemological debate. However, to some extent this argument is irrelevant, since it is by no means clear that the approaches *do* have different bases. As I have indicated at several points in this book, claims for such fundamental differences often turn out to be empty. Much as the critical Marxist position may suggest that conventional sociology of knowledge is 'empiricist', it is actually difficult to sustain a non-empiricist position in practice.[6] Similarly, Berger and Luckmann's ontological claims about the autonomy of the human subject tend not to be so radical when worked out in detail. Practice does not always live up to the epistemological programme.

In some ways the epistemological and ontological *problems* faced by the three approaches have some similarities even if solutions do differ. Thus all three are forced to formulate a view of science and to take a position on the place of the human subject in relation to determining social structures.

A number of the writers reviewed in this book have felt that any sociological analysis of knowledge necessitates a sharp distinction between science and ideology. In one of his phases, Mannheim suggests that science and mathematics should be seen as exempt from social causation. Althusser argues that science is an autonomous practice. In Schutz's work, the distinction appears as one between scientific practice and everyday life, two quite distinct provinces of meaning, with radically different cognitive styles. Now, it is important to have a clear conception of scientific practice, for it is only such a conception that will enable one to *recognize* ideology. However, this is a very different claim from that which wishes to separate out science as a category of knowledge from other knowledge which is ideological, because science has to be exempt from social causation, while ideology does not. To show that science is rooted in social practices is not to show that it is false.[7] Thus a sociology of knowledge does not have to operate with the assumption of an autonomous science, even if it may choose to *concentrate* on ideologies because those happen to be sociologically most interesting.

Another problem systematic to all sociological theories of knowledge is that allegedly created by seeing social structures as 'giving' consciousness to individuals. Just as the very explanation of knowledge in social terms seems to cast doubt on its validity, so the same attempt seems to imply limitations on the human freedom to think. Again, this is not a difficulty confined to the sociology of knowledge. A great deal of debate in sociology generally is concerned with the relationship that social structures have to / individuals.

Within the conventional sociology of knowledge, there is often a temptation to resolve the tension between the autonomy of the individual consciousness and the determining properties of the social structure, by postulating some area that is not social. Just as Mannheim suggested in his early work that there were areas of knowledge, such as science, that are not socially determined, others have argued that there is some irreducible component of the human mind that is independent of social factors. As Stark points out in his book *The Sociology of Knowledge*: 'In the literature, the problem has very often been seen in terms of such a dividing line between an area of determined and an area of free thought, and the concrete questions asked have then been concerned with the correct placing of some given set of concepts in relation to this dividing line.'[8] Stark argues that such a solution is not adequate, for social determination is at the root of all thinking, most basically because language, without which thought is impossible, is uniquely social. In his later work, Mannheim would undoubtedly have approved of such an argument, asserting that there is no non-social province.

Stark, however, still believes that there is a problem but his solution is muddled in a way characteristic of the conventional sociology of knowledge within which he largely works. Thus he suggests that he does not want to be accused of advocating determinism: 'By insisting in this way that *all* human thinking is dependent on social reality . . . we are not of course propagating any kind of determinism in the narrower, quasi-mechanical sense of the word. . . . Not even the Marxists have cast serious doubt upon the true spontaneity of human thought.'[9] Asking, then, how one can reconcile such apparent indeterminacy with the whole enterprise of the sociology of knowledge, Stark provides two kinds of answer. First, he argues that societies do not determine completely the patterns of belief in a society, since there is considerable diversity in such patterns in fact. This, however, will not answer his question, since the assertion of diversity, or the assertion of the existence of patterns of belief not associated with class, does not establish the importance of the autonomy or 'spontaneity' of the human consciousness; diversity could well be explained purely in social structural terms. Second, Stark suggests that men do break out of the confines of social determination by thinking outside the categories characteristic of their social group. Nonetheless, this is not the assertion of asocial intellect, since such persons will always adopt a new socially established 'vantage point from which to survey reality'. However, again, this is no solution since the problem is not one of the behaviour of the exceptional individual, but of the relationship of the individual consciousness in general to social structure.

The difficulties attaching to the formulation of this relationship in the conventional sociology of knowledge attract criticism from phenomenologically oriented sociologists of knowledge. It will be remembered that writers such as Berger and Luckmann criticize conventional sociology for relying too heavily on a conception of society giving a consciousness to individuals, and neglecting the processes by which individuals actively create their own consciousness of the world. Despite these criticisms, however, the phenomenological account of the relationship between structure and individual consciousness is a somewhat peculiar one. Whatever the protestations of Schutz, Berger and Luckmann, social structure emerges as a powerful and constraining force. Their arguments, as they are practically worked out, tend to sacrifice a large measure of the autonomy of the individual consciousness, as I have tried to show in the preceding two chapters. This sacrifice seriously undermines the radicalism of their programme and takes the edge off their criticisms of the conventional position. In addition, they have a problem in explaining where the autonomy of the individual consciousness comes from. Too often, the principle of autonomy is simply asserted. Nonetheless, it must have a cause of some kind. Does autonomy perhaps lie in some intrinsic and invariant property of the human mind? Alternatively, since this does seem a foolish question, does one *need* to explain autonomy independently of structural conditions? Thus, autonomy may simply mean relative independence of a set of structural conditions at a particular time, but a causal dependence on structural conditions in the past.

Autonomy is not some invariant human essence, but is a quality dependent on structural factors. Such a formulation is, indeed, not dissimilar to Berger and Luckmann's model of the process of institutionalization.

There are similar problems, in reverse, for the critique from the contemporary Marxist theory of ideology. I have already noted the hostility of this school to any attempt to 'reduce' ideology to the human subject or even to social classes. Ideology is seen, not as proceeding from a knowing subject; 'ideology has conditions of existence which cannot be "read off" from the place of the subject in the relations of production'.[10] Ideology is a structural category, whose explanation lies in other structural categories, not in some unexplained autonomy of the individual consciousness. Human subjects do not have an ontological priority as essences from which everything else is derived; they are 'constituted' at least partly by ideology. Such a view, totally at variance with both the conventional sociology of knowledge, and the phenomenological school, has the advantage of avoiding the inconsistencies and ambiguities of those approaches. However it also carries with it its own disadvantages. For example, Althusser's earlier work may have the effect of reducing the theoretical importance of the human subject, but there is still the requirement for *some* theory of the place of the subject. Otherwise, his account has a tendency 'to reduce the subject to its place in the social formation; and to endow that subject with all the (untheorized) faculties necessary for it to obtain, through its experience, the consciousness appropriate to that place'.[11] In his later work, Althusser does offer the beginnings of a theory of the mechanism that connects ideology and the human subject by trying to show how ideology has the effect of 'constituting' subjects.[12]

The Conventional Sociology of Knowledge and the Critique from Marxism

The central concept of the conventional sociology of knowledge is that of 'social location'. Belief is said to be correlated with social location, which can take a variety of forms with class being most commonly stressed. Such a very general approach has generated a wide range of studies. Thus Mannheim relates nineteenth-century conservative thought to the social location of the nobility.[13] Seeman discusses the relationship between ethnic minority status and intellectual perspectives.[14] Dibble investigates the relationship between occupations and ideologies.[15] All these studies, and others, are essentially arguing that a particular social location produces a particular set of basic assumptions. They undoubtedly add to our knowledge of the social world even if there is not much integration between studies which might produce general theory. One of the chief difficulties in the way of such a theory is the lack of a mechanism which will *explain* the discovered correlation. That is, we need to know why a particular social group takes up one particular form of thought rather than another. Occasionally, an explanation is provided which practically takes the form of suggesting that members of a group adopt particular forms of knowledge as a matter of conscious decision. Merton's analysis of the relationship of seventeenth-century science and the demands of the economy is a case in point.[16] Merton argues that the scientists associated with the Royal Society investigated such problems as the measurement of longitude at sea in response to a capitalist economy's demand for efficient marine transport. However, the mechanism connecting scientific investigation with the demands of the economy is very direct. Scientists, in need of public approval and royal patronage, decided to apply themselves to practical problems, and were most definitely encouraged to do so by Charles II. Connections as direct as this are not sociologically mysterious. What is of much greater interest are those cases in which very basic intellectual assumptions or world-views are shaped *unawares* by social location.

I have argued that the more Marxist variants of the conventional sociology of knowledge effectively use the concept of interest as the explanatory mechanism connecting social location and form of belief. Classes, for example, will have particular ideologies shaped in response to their particular interests. Such a notion can work well. In Part I(3), I have tried to show how the particular concepts of individualism can be explained in terms of the class-interests of a capitalist class in its specific economic practice. As a general theory, however, it has its weaknesses. In particular, it is not good at explaining the ideologies of certain social classes like the nobility of early nineteenth-century Germany, since it is not clear how their economic practices generate specific interests which produce particular ideologies which are 'appropriate' to the economic practices. Even more acutely, in the conventional Marxist scheme, it is difficult to see how social groups which are not classes have interests which mould specific forms of belief. In what sense, for example, do generations have interests which 'produce' ideologies? If concepts of such interests cannot be produced, what mechanism explains why generation groups adopt particular ideologies, which would go beyond the mere correlation of generation with ideology?

One possible solution to these problems is to argue that so far interests have been conceived too narrowly, simply in terms of economic practices dictated by a class's participation in an economy.[17] Thus, a capitalist class has an interest in adopting individualist beliefs because these beliefs permit and encourage economic activity based on free markets. This, however, produces a view of interest which is ahistorical and, in a way, asocial. In fact, the economic practices of social classes are not conducted in a social vacuum, but in a relationship to other classes and social forces. Hence, the interests of a class must be seen, not as fixed by economic requirements, but as conditioned by an overall social situation, which includes economic practice and the relationship with other classes amongst other things. With such a view of interest there seems no reason in principle not to extend it to social groups other than classes. Many such groups, such as ethnic minorities, generations, or women, will have relationships, and relationships of conflict at that, with other social groups. The difficulty, however, is that such an extension of the concept of interest will make the concept so general and vague that it loses all explanatory power. As always, the test must be: do *particular* interests, formed in particular social situations, produce *particular* and *appropriate* forms of belief?

The critical Marxist perspective outlined in Part II can be seen both as an advance on, and as a criticism of, the conventional account. Generally in this formulation, classes cannot be seen as the origin of knowledge since that origin lies deeper in the social structure in the mode of production. The problem is, then, that the concept of class is not fundamental enough.[18] Plainly, such a view is an attack on the concept of social location, central to the conventional sociology of knowledge. It is effectively suggested that what is missing from the conventional account is a view of those structural factors that construct particular locations, and it is in these structural factors that the origin of particular beliefs lies. This argument will apply not only to social classes, but to any social group taken to be the social base for a system of belief. Mannheim, for example, whatever his reliance on Marx, had a tendency to attribute systems of belief to social groups which were not otherwise structurally located. Thus, he saw social classes as locked in struggle with one another but not as produced by other structural elements. Generations, likewise, had specific systems of belief, but were not seen as *socially* defined, having, if anything, a biological base.

The critical Marxist position, then, takes ideology as a concept formulable at the level of the mode of production, considered as a set of *underlying* structures, rather than at the level of class or social group. At this underlying level, ideology functions as a *condition of existence* of the economy. The formulation of this concept of ideological condition of existence discussed in Part II(5) is a definite advance on the conventional Marxist conceptions of base and superstructure, except that it tends to conceive of the relationship between ideology and economy too strictly. Thus, it does not seem possible to me to argue that particular economies (or modes of production) require given ideological forms. It is true that economies may require 'extra-economic' forms for their adequate functioning, and the nature of these forms may typically vary as between different modes of production. However, there is no reason to suppose that *particular* ideologies are required, that political structures cannot perform the required functions equally well, or, even, that *ideological* forms need to be present at all.[19]

However, even if a rather weakened form of the notion that ideological systems function as conditions of existence of economies was advanced, there is still an analytical problem to be resolved. Ideologies do not produce themselves; they have to be produced and then permit or encourage particular economic practices. The question is then: how are ideologies produced? The answer is that class formations, or their functional equivalent, generate ideological forms which are functional for economic practices. By class formation I mean a class, or class alliance, or social group. The relationships can be summarized diagram-matically as follows:[20]

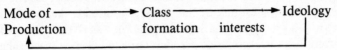

Three points must be made in commentary. First, I have over-simplified the relationships involved in the diagram since, amongst other things, the way that a class formation is created itself has an impact on the constitution of a mode of production.[21] Second, societies are rarely characterized by the presence of one single mode of production. Modes will exist in relations of domination, subordination, co-operation, or conflict, and this complexity will have effects in a more complex class structure and a more diverse array of ideological forms. In sum, it is not just that modes of production represent fundamental social structures underlying the social locations of conventional sociology of knowledge, it is also that the relationships between modes determine the relationships between classes and the relationships between ideological forms. Third, it is not necessarily the case that a social class stands in a one-to-one relationship to a mode of production. As I have said, a class formation consists of a class or, perhaps more typically, alliances between classes, or other social groups. This is a welcome corrective to the view, often represented within the conventional sociology of knowledge, that a particular ideology 'belongs' to a particular class.

The Quality of Belief

Even the suggestion that it is class formations that 'produce' ideology conceals further questions. As I have argued in Part II(6), it is important to formulate both the means by which more theoretical knowledge is produced, and the means by which all forms of belief are distributed. As Mannheim indicated, at least in one of his phases, intellectuals have a variable relationship to social classes, and at times may function independently of any class. Thus, an analysis of *some* forms of belief may demand an account of the role of the intellectual stratum, in addition to the social elements mentioned in the diagram. A case in point is the analysis of individualism in seventeenth, eighteenth and nineteenth century England. To the extent that this was theoretical construction, as in the political philosophy of the period, we need to know how and why it was produced, and what its relation was to the more diffuse conceptions (and economic practices) of a much wider social class.

Important as these questions are, an excessive interest in intellectuals and intellectualized belief is a weakness of the conventional sociology of knowledge. Of much greater importance is the way that idelologies are represented and diffused in the relatively untheoretical 'ways of life' of whole social groups. It is notably difficult to provide a way of identifying these 'ways of life', or common-sense beliefs, and providing substantive studies of them, and this is a major task of a sociology of knowledge.[22] Writers in the phenomenological school, however, go further than this in their attempt to construct the object of the sociology of knowledge. To some extent, their conception of this object includes what Neisser calls 'practical knowledge' which is 'the human know-how that is not based on a systematic knowledge of the laws governing nature or society but, though obtained pragmatically, possesses a high degree of certainty: for example, how to till the soil, how to make simple tools, how to care for a herd, how to hunt. . . .'[23] Beyond this, Schutz and Berger and Luckmann argue that the proper concern of the sociology of knowledge is 'everything that passes for knowledge in society' in particular that knowledge appropriate to everyday life such as the knowledge each of us has of other people. I have argued in Part III(7) and (8) that the characterization of knowledge offered by these writers is in fact a partial one. It emphasizes the everyday life-world as a place typically without doubt, or questioning, and stresses the knowledge held in common by all men, rather than that which differs as between groups of men. The result is an 'anthropological' conception of common-sense tied to constants of human nature. It is difficult to tell whether this distortion is intrinsic to the phenomenological method. It is certainly the case that analysis of the everyday life-world *can* produce results that are sociologically interesting, but it also produces a great deal that is trivial and it has not led to any real advance in the sociology of knowledge.

Many writers in the critical Marxist school also quarrel with the identification of the object of the sociology of knowledge (or ideology) provided by the conventional approach to the subject. They suggest that ideology denotes a *reality* that is not captured by referring to ideology either as mental or as a false consciousness. Actually there are two related claims here. Thus it may be objected to the notion of beliefs as 'mental' phenomena carried around in people's heads, merely ideas, that this misses the critical way in which these beliefs are really ways of life or ideological practices. However this view essentially collapses ideological practices into other practices and robs the ideological of any distinctiveness. Second, it is argued that ideologies cannot be said to be straightforwardly false, in the sense in which they do not correspond with 'reality'. For example, fetishized beliefs are not false in this sense, because people must hold them in order to live in a society based on commodity production.[24] However, I have argued in various parts of the book that to take such a view of ideology or belief as 'real' is to limit the theory of ideology and the sociology of knowledge. We need theories of beliefs as illusions as well. Indeed, as against both the contemporary theory of ideology and the conventional sociology of knowledge, one needs a sociology of knowledge that shows how beliefs about the world are distorting in very *different* ways.

Notes

INTRODUCTION

[1] See R. K. Merton, 'The Sociology of Knowledge' in his *Social Theory and Social Structure* (New York: The Free Press, 1957), J. E. Curtis and J. W. Petras (eds.), *The Sociology of Knowledge* (London: Duckworth, 1970), G. W. Remmling (ed.), *Towards the Sociology of Knowledge* (London: Routledge and Kegan Paul, 1973), J. Plamenatz, *Ideology* (London: Macmillan, 1971), P. Hamilton, *Knowledge and Social Structure* (London: Routledge and Kegan Paul, 1974).

[2] P. Berger and T. Luckmann, *The Social Construction of Reality* (London: Allen Lane, 1967).

[3] Merton, *op. cit.*, p. 456.

[4] J. Macquet, *The Sociology of Knowledge* (Westport: Greenwood Press, 1951), pp. 255-6.

[5] Berger and Luckmann, *op. cit.*, p. 15 (author's italics).

[6] E. Shils, 'The Concept and Function of Ideology', *International Encyclopaedia of the Social Sciences* (New York: Macmillan, 1968), p. 66.

[7] *Ibid.*, p. 68.

[8] D. Apter, 'Ideology and Discontent', in D. Apter (ed.), *Ideology and Discontent* (New York: The Free Press, 1964). Apter's comments on ideology are intended to be merely suggestive and a developed theory would have to specify in a great deal more detail the mechanisms by which ideology and solidarity are linked. Further, the relationship between the solidarity and identity aspects of the function of ideology is vague. This latter question is regarded by C. Geertz ('Ideology as a Cultural System' in Apter, *op. cit.*) as an important one, for he seems to argue that the social and personality dimensions are analytically linked and that consequently any satisfactory functionalist theory of ideology must be a socio-psychological one. Thus, in what he describes as the 'strain theory', ideology is a response to social strain, which is a fundamental and

necessary characteristic of human societies which are all riddled with 'insoluble antimonies'. Further, friction or strain does not just appear on the social level, it is also characteristic of the individual psyche. As Geertz elegantly says, 'In the modern world at least, most men live lives of patterned desperation.'

[9] For a further discussion of these distinctions see N. Harris, *Beliefs in Society* (London: Watts and Co. 1968) and D. Miller, 'Ideology and the problem of false consciousness', *Political Studies*, vol. 20, no. 4 (1972).

[10] Plamenatz, *op. cit.*, p. 15.

[11] *Ibid.*, p. 17.

[12] Chiefly D. Bell, S. Lipset and E. Shils. See C. Waxman, *The End of Ideology Debate* (New York: Funk and Wagnalls, 1968).

[13] D. Bell, *The End of Ideology* (New York: The Free Press, 1962), p. 402.

[14] A. Lovejoy, *The Great Chain of Being* (New York: Harper and Row, 1936). For a similar view of the history of ideas see G. Boas, *The History of Ideas* (New York: Charles Scribner's Sons, 1969). For a somewhat different view see J. Dunn, 'The identity of the history of ideas', *Philosophy*, vol. 43, no. 164 (1968) and Q. Skinner, 'Meaning and Understanding in the History of Ideas', *History and Theory*, vol. 8, no. 1 (1969).

[15] Lovejoy, *op. cit.*

[16] For an example of this, see the debate over 'internalist' and 'externalist' histories of science in G. Basalla (ed.), *The Rise of Modern Science* (Lexington, Mass.: Heath, 1968).

[17] Lovejoy, *op. cit.*, p. 15.

[18] F. Bacon, selections from the *Novum Organum* reprinted in Curtis and Petras (eds.), *op. cit.*

[19] *Ibid.*, p. 89.

[20] *Ibid.*, p. 93.

[21] *Ibid.*, p. 90.

[22] *Ibid.*, p. 90.

[23] E. Durkheim, *The Elementary Forms of the Religious Life* (London: Allen and Unwin, 1964), p. 10.

[24] *Ibid.*, p. 11.

[25] *Ibid.*, p. 16.

PART I: 1. MARXISM: THE CONVENTIONAL ACCOUNT

[1] See, for example, K. Marx and F. Engels, *The German Ideology* (London: Lawrence and Wishart, 1965), K. Marx, *Poverty of Philosophy* (London: Lawrence and Wishart) and *The Communist Manifesto* in K.

Marx and F. Engels, *Selected Works* (London: Lawrence and Wishart, 1970).

[2] Marx, *German Ideology*, p. 30.

[3] *Ibid.*, p. 38.

[4] K. Marx, Preface to *A Contribution to the Critique of Political Economy*, in Marx and Engels, *Selected Works*, p. 181.

[5] K. Marx, *The Eighteenth Brumaire of Louis Bonaparte*, in Marx and Engels, *Selected Works*, p. 117.

[6] Actually Marx does not always use the word 'determined'. In *The German Ideology*, for example, he speaks of ideas being *interwoven* with or being the *emanation* of 'material activity'.

[7] Marx and Engels, *German Ideology*, *op. cit.*, p. 270.

[8] 'And as in private life one differentiates between what a man thinks and says of himself and what he really is and does, so in historical struggles one must distinguish still more the phrases and fancies of parties from their real organism and their real interests.' Marx, *The Eighteenth Brumaire of Louis Bonaparte*, pp. 117-8.

[9] But for a contrary view see W. G. Runciman, 'False Consciousness', *Philosophy*, vol. 44, no. 170 (1966). I am indebted in my discussion at this point to W. E. Connolly, 'On "Interests" in Politics', *Politics and Society*, vol. 2, no. 4 (1972) and S. Lukes, *Power* (London: Macmillan, 1974).

[10] Connolly, *op. cit.*, p. 472.

[11] *Ibid.*, p. 472.

[12] Marx and Engels, *German Ideology*, p. 214.

[13] Compare J. Szacki, 'Some remarks on the Marxian concept of false consciousness', *Polish Sociological Bulletin*, vol. 14 (1966) with Runciman, *op. cit.*

[14] Marx, Preface to *A Contribution to the Critique of Political Economy*, p. 181.

[15] C. W. Mills, *The Marxists* (Harmondsworth: Penguin Books, 1963), p. 82.

[16] G. D. H. Cole, *The Meaning of Marxism* (Ann Arbor: University of Michigan Press, 1964), p. 55.

[17] F. Engels, Letter to Starkenburg in K. Marx and F. Engels, *Selected Correspondence* (Moscow: Progress Publishers, 1955), p. 466ff.

[18] K. Marx, *Capital* (London: Lawrence and Wishart, 1970), p. 234. See the more extended discussion in the whole of Chapter 10 of *Capital*.

[19] Engels in a letter to Bloch in Marx and Engels, *Selected Works*, p. 682.

[20] J. Plamenatz, *Ideology* (London: Macmillan, 1971) and *Man and Society* (London: Longmans Green, 1963), vol. 2, pp. 269-408.

[21] G. Cohen, 'On some criticisms of historical materialism', *Sup-*

plementary Proceedings of the Aristotelian Society, vol. 44 (1970), pp. 121–41.

[22] Marx and Engels, *German Ideology*, p. 61.

[23] See Part I(B) and Part II. Mannheim's discussion of the role of intellectuals is of particular importance.

[24] For an expansion of the following argument see N. Abercrombie and B. Turner, 'The dominant ideology thesis', *British Journal of Sociology*, vol. 29, no. 2 (1978).

[25] See, for example, M. Mann, *Consciousness and Action in the Western Working Class* (London: Macmillan, 1973) and F. Parkin, *Class Inequality and Political Order* (London: Paladin, 1972).

[26] I would want to argue, following Abercrombie and Turner, *op. cit.*, that in contemporary capitalism there is no *requirement* for a property-owining class for the preservation, transmission and accumulation of capital. Essentially these functions have been taken over by various institutions outside the family although, of course, an unequal ownership of property may be the effect of the continued private appropriation of profit. Since I have suggested that the dominant ideology functions chiefly for the coherence of the dominant class, one might expect that in contemporary capitalism there is a less well marked dominant ideology. I suggest that all the evidence suggests that this is the case.

[27] D. Apter, 'Ideology and Discontent', in D. Apter (ed.); *Ideology and Discontent* (New York: The Free Press, 1964).

PART I: 2. MANNHEIM

[1] K. Mannheim, 'Preliminary Approach to the Problem', in his *Ideology and Utopia* (London: Routledge and Kegan Paul, 1960), p. 48.

[2] Merton is somewhat guilty of this. See R. K. Merton, 'Karl Mannheim and the Sociology of Knowledge', in his *Social Theory and Social Structure* (New York: The Free Press, 1957).

[3] Mannheim, 'Ideology and Utopia', in his *Ideology and Utopia*, p. 51.

[4] K. Mannheim, 'The Problem of the Sociology of Knowledge', in his *Essays on the Sociology of Knowledge* (London: Routledge and Kegan Paul, 1952), p. 181.

[5] Mannheim, 'Ideology and Utopia', p. 104.

[6] K. Mannheim, 'The Ideological and the Sociological Interpretation of Intellectual Phenomena', in K. Wolff (ed.), *From Karl Mannheim* (New York: Oxford University Press, 1971).

[7] *Ibid.*, pp. 116–7.

[8] *Ibid.*, p. 119.

[9] Mannheim, 'The Problem of the Sociology of Knowledge', p. 181.

[10] K. Mannheim, 'Towards the Sociology of the Mind', in his *Essays on the Sociology of Culture* (London: Routledge and Kegan Paul, 1956), p. 27.

[11] Mannheim, 'Preliminary Approach to the Problem', pp. 2–3.

[12] K. Mannheim, 'On the Interpretation of Weltanschauung', in his *Essays on the Sociology of Knowledge*.

[13] *Ibid.*, p. 33.

[14] *Ibid.*, p. 46.

[15] *Ibid.*, p. 47.

[16] G. W. Remmling, *The Sociology of Karl Mannheim* (London: Routledge and Kegan Paul, 1975), p. 25.

[17] Mannheim, 'On the Interpretation of Weltanschauung', p. 73.

[18] Mannheim, 'Ideology and Utopia', pp. 247–8.

[19] Mannheim, 'The Problem of Generations', in his *Essays on the Sociology of Knowledge*, pp. 286–7.

[20] *Ibid.*, p. 290.

[21] Mannheim, 'Ideology and Utopia', p. 248.

[22] Mannheim, 'Preliminary Approach to the Problem', p. 36.

[23] Mannheim, 'Ideology and Utopia', p. 175. Situationally congruous ideas are those informed by a properly sociological consciousness.

[24] *Ibid.*, p. 187.

[25] *Ibid.*, p. 179.

[26] Mannheim, 'Competition as a Cultural Phenomenon', in his *Essays on the Sociology of Knowledge* (London: Routledge and Kegan Paul, 1954).

[27] *Ibid.*, pp. 196–7.

[28] For example, 'As the fundamental trend of economic and intellectual progress moves along, strata which began by being progressive may become conservative after they have achieved their ambition; strata which at a time played a leading role may suddenly feel impelled to go into opposition against the dominant trend' ('The Problem of the Sociology of Knowledge', pp. 985–6).

[29] J. Heeren, 'Karl Mannheim and the Intellectual Elite, *British Journal of Sociology*, vol. 22, no. 1 (March 1971).

[30] Mannheim, 'The Problem of the Sociology of Knowledge', p. 183.

[31] *Ibid.*, p. 135.

[32] Mannheim, 'Competition as a Cultural Phenomenon', p. 194.

[33] Mannheim, 'Ideology and Utopia', pp. 70–1.

[34] *Ibid.*, p. 76.

[35] Mannheim, 'The Sociology of Knowledge', in his *Ideology and Utopia*, p. 253.

[36] *Ibid.*, p. 264.

[37] Merton, 'The Sociology of Knowledge', in his *Social Theory and Social Structure*.

[38] K. Mannheim, 'Conservative Thought', in his *Essays on Sociology and Social Psychology* (London: Routledge and Kegan Paul, 1963), p. 53.

[39] *Ibid.*, p. 114.

[40] See *ibid.*, pp. 116–19.

[41] *Ibid.*, p. 86.

[42] *Ibid.*, p. 87.

[43] *Ibid.*, p. 127.

[44] *Ibid.*, p. 88.

[45] See, for example, the section on Mannheim in I. M. Zeitlin, *Ideology and the Development of Sociological Theory* (Englewood-Cliffs: Prentice-Hall, 1968).

[46] See R. Keat and J. Urry, *Social Theory as Science* (London: Routledge and Kegan Paul, 1975).

PART I: 3. SOME DIFFICULTIES IN THE CONVENTIONAL POSITION

[1] J. Macquet, *The Sociology of Knowledge* (Westport: Greenwood Press, 1951), p. 5.

[2] R. K. Merton, *Social Theory and Social Structure* (New York: The Free Press, 1957), p. 460.

[3] G. Gurvitch, *The Social Frameworks of Knowledge* (Oxford: Basil Blackwell, 1971), p. 89.

[4] For a good summary of Scheler's position see W. Stark, *The Sociology of Knowledge* (London: Routledge and Kegan Paul, 1958), p. 77.

[5] For an account of Sorokin's views see Macquet, *op. cit.*

[6] See S. Lukes, *Individualism* (Oxford: Basil Blackwell, 1973) for an introductory discussion.

[7] D. J. Manning, *Liberalism* (London: J. M. Dent and Sons, 1976), p. 14.

[8] L. Goldmann, *The Philosophy of the Enlightenment* (London: Routledge and Kegan Paul, 1973).

[9] *Ibid.*, p. 18.

[10] *Ibid.*, p. 18.

[11] *Ibid.*, p. 20.

[12] C. B. MacPherson, *The Political Theory of Possessive Individualism* (Oxford: Oxford University Press 1964), p. 231.

'The individual was seen neither as a moral whole, nor as part of a larger whole, but as an owner of himself. The relation of ownership, having become for more and more men the critically important relation determining their actual freedom and actual prospect of realizing their full potentialities, was read back into the nature of the individual. The individual . . . is free inasmuch as he is proprietor of his person and capacities. The human essence is freedom from dependence on the wills of others, and freedom is a function of possession. Society becomes a lot of free equal individuals related to each other as proprietors of their own capacities and of what they have acquired by their exercise. Society consists of relations of exchange between proprietors' (*ibid.*, p. 3).

[13] *Ibid.*, p. 270.

[14] I. Watt, *The Rise of the Novel* (Harmondsworth: Penguin Books, 1963).

[15] *Ibid.*, p. 13.

[16] *Ibid.*, p. 14.

[17] *Ibid.*, p. 15.

[18] *Ibid.*, p. 32.

[19] I. Watt, 'Robinson Crusoe as a myth', in E. and T. Burns (eds.), *Sociology of Literature and Drama* (Harmondsworth: Penguin Books, 1973).

[20] Watt's *The Rise of the Novel* can be used to demonstrate a relationship between the development of capitalism and the appearance of the novel form in the eighteenth century. I have presented the relationship mostly in terms of the manner in which the concept of individualism is central to the concerns of the novel and important for the development of capitalism as an economic system. Swingewood (Chapter 8 of D. Laurenson and A. Swingewood, *The Sociology of Literature*, London: Paladin, 1972) advances an objection to the inclusion of Fielding in Watt's thesis, an objection which is interesting because it also serves to clarify the overall argument of *The Rise of the Novel*.

Swingewood argues that in many important respects Fielding's novels *are* like those of Defoe and Richardson. *Tom Jones*, for example, uses most of the narrative techniques discussed above. There are however, some important departures. Fielding was a little more inclined to write of general types and to use names reminiscent of eternal human qualities such as Allworthy. However the main differences between Fielding on the one hand and Defoe and Richardson on the other lie in content rather than form. Thus Fielding very much thought in terms of an opposition between country and town. Country life stood for all that was good and wholesome, while the town was generally a place of evil. For the other two writers there was little indication that there was any moral difference between town and country. Again, for Fielding, birth and social position is of great importance. Ultimately, it was Jones's apparently lowly birth that was responsible for his eviction from Allworthy's house, and the discovery that he was in fact of rather higher birth that led to his restoration. Neither Defoe nor Richardson value the social position given by birth in quite this way. However, the feature that most significantly differentiates Fielding from Defoe and Richardson is the *kind* of hero that the former writes about.

I argued earlier that Crusoe was a hero who intervened in the world; he actively tried to mould events to suit his purposes. Tom Jones, on the other hand, 'is rarely called upon to exercise any form of initiative, and his progression through the novel is wholly the result of the unintended consequences of his actions and does not flow from his personal efforts: things happen to Jones and he accepts his fate with resignation and humour' (p. 193). Tom Jones is thus essentially passive in the face of the world. Events control him; he does not control events.

Swingewood suggests that the differences between Fielding and, say, Richardson, amount to the presentation of two quite different world-views which are appropriate to different social classes. Richardson expresses the view of an ascending bourgeoisie, while Fielding represents the small gentry, at that time in fairly rapid decline. If these classes correspond in some way to modes of production, then the argument is that Fielding's version of the novel form does not 'match' the capitalist mode of production.

[21] Watt, *op. cit.*, p. 62.

[22] See, for example, the debate surrounding Weber's *The Protestant Ethic and the Spirit of Capitalism*, in R. W. Green (ed.), *Protestantism and Capitalism* (New York: Heath, 1959).

[23] Manning, *op. cit.*, p. 14.

[24] Goldmann, *op. cit.*, p. 51.

[25] A. Gamble (*The Conservative Nation*, London: Routledge and Kegan Paul, 1974) for example, argues that, since the Second World War, political debate has been conducted within the framework of what he calls the 'welfare consensus'. This consensus has been anti-individualist at least in the sense that it permits the State to place constraints on individual action and its origins lie in the belief that *laissez-faire* capitalism has generated more problems than it has solved. Of course, it would be dangerous to argue that late capitalism differs from early capitalism in that it has completely replaced individualist doctrines; there is, despite the welfare consensus, still widespread agreement on the fundamental rights of individual property, for example. Further, one could hardly argue that individualist doctrines have entirely disappeared from political debate, although it may be suggested that they, yet again, have an essentially *oppositional* character in their dissent from the welfare consensus.

[26] K. Marx and F. Engels, *The German Ideology* (London: Lawrence and Wishart, 1968).

[27] R. Williams, 'Base and Superstructure in Marxist Cultural Theory', *New Left Review*, no. 82 (November–December 1973), pp. 3–16.

[28] It might be that the fact of decline may be more important than anything else in shaping the world-view of a particular class; classes, similarly placed in an order of domination might be compared although

they were located in different modes of production. For example the tragic vision identified by Goldmann (*The Hidden God*, London: Routledge and Kegan Paul, 1964) as the essential constituent of the works of Racine and Pascal, is not dissimilar to the sense of fate in the contemporary novels of Waugh and Powell.

[29] Ironically this conservative social diagnosis is well represented in Mannheim's later work. See, for example, his *Man and Society in an Age of Reconstruction* (London: Kegan Paul, 1940).

[30] See K. Mannheim *Freedom, Power, and Democratic Planning* (London: Routledge, 1951).

[31] For example, the poetry of thirties writers such as Auden and McNiece, who are often thought of as typically socialist, in fact displays some characteristic conservative themes, such as the importance of aesthetic value, the vice of disorder, and the danger of mass-society.

[32] For other treatments of conservatism from very different viewpoints see P. W. Buck (ed.), *How Conservatives Think* (Harmondsworth: Penguin Books, 1975), S. Giner, *Mass-Society* (London: Martin Robertson, 1976), N. Sullivan, *Conservatism* (London: Dent, 1976), A. Gamble, *The Conservative Nation*, op. cit.

[33] At least not within the sociology of knowledge. There is however a growing literature on images of the class structure. See M. Bulmer (ed.), *Working Class Images of Society* (London: Routledge, 1975) and K. Roberts *et al.*, *The Fragmentary Class Structure* (London: Heinemann, 1977).

[34] See Z. Bauman, *Hermeneutics and Social Science* (London: Hutchinson, 1979).

PART II: 4. THE NATURE OF IDEOLOGY

[1] A. Gramsci, *Prison Notebooks* (London: Lawrence and Wishart, 1976) edited by Q. Hoare and G. Nowell-Smith, p. 323.

[2] *Ibid.*, p. 419.

[3] *Ibid.*, p. 333.

[4] F. Parkin, *Class Inequality and Political Order* (London: Paladin, 1971), pp. 94–5.

[5] See M. Mann, *Consciousness and Action among the Western Working Class* (London: Macmillan, 1973), esp. Chapter 6. 'Thus, studies of working class attitudes which rely on questions posed in general and non-situational terms are likely to produce findings which emphasize class consensus on values; this is because the dominant value system will tend to provide the moral frame of reference. Conversely, studies which specify particular social contexts of belief and action . . . are likely to find more

evidence for a class differentiated value system; this is because in situational contexts of choice and action, the subordinate value system will tend to provide the moral frame of reference' (Parkin, *op. cit.*, p. 95).

[6] R. Hoggart, *The Uses of Literacy* (Harmondsworth: Penguin Books, 1968).

[7] *Ibid.*, p. 29.

[8] R. Barthes, *Elements of Semiology* (London: Cape, 1969), and *Mythologies*, (London: Paladin, 1976).

[9] Barthes, *Mythologies*, p. 116.

[10] See particularly, L. Althusser, 'Ideology and Ideological State Apparatuses', in his *Lenin and Philosophy* (London: New Left Books, 1971), p. 149ff. and also his essay, 'On the Materialist Dialectic', in *For Marx* (Harmondsworth: Penguin Books, 1966). For further discussion see Conclusion.

[11] Althusser, 'Ideology and Ideological State Apparatuses', p. 157.

[12] Althusser writes that actions are inserted into practices and writes further of the believing subject that 'his ideas are his material actions inserted into material practices governed by material rituals which are themselves defined by the material ideological apparatus from which derive the ideas of that subject' ('Ideology and Ideological State Apparatuses', p. 158).

[13] I am greatly indebted in this section to the excellent discussions of the subject in N. Geras, 'Fetishism in Marx's Capital', *New Left Review*, no. 65 (January/February 1971) and J. Mepham, 'The theory of ideology in Capital', *Radical Philosophy*, no. 2 (1972).

[14] Mepham, *op. cit.*

[15] M. Godelier, 'System, Structure, and Contradiction in Capital', *Socialist Register*, 1967. Quoted in Geras, *op. cit.*, p. 79.

[16] Though it is important to beware of the Hegelian connotations of speaking of *essence* and appearance.

[17] See S. Hall, 'Rethinking the "base and superstructure" metaphor', in J. Bloomfield, *Class, Hegemony, and Party* (London: Lawrence and Wishart, 1977), Geras, *op. cit.*, N. Rose, 'Fetishism and ideology; a review of theoretical proboems', *Ideology and Consciousness*, no. 2 (Autumn 1977), and G. McLennan, V. Molina and R. Peters, 'Althusser's theory of ideology', *Working Papers in Cultural Studies*, no. 10 (Birmingham: Centre for Cultural Studies, 1977).

[18] Hall, *op. cit.*, p. 62.

[19] K. Marx, *Capital* (London: Lawrence and Wishart, 1970), vol. 3, p. 830.

[20] *Ibid.*, vol. 1, p. 176.

[21] *Ibid.*, p. 540.

[22] *Ibid.*, p. 307, quoted in Geras, *op. cit.*, p. 69.

[23] I am very grateful to Brian Longhurst and Ken Smith for our discussions on commodity fetishism.

[24] To go beyond this text can be theoretically foolhardy. Marx may use the word 'fetishism' fairly frequently but it is by no means clear that he denotes the same concept each time.

[25] Marx, *Capital*, vol. 1, p. 71.

[26] *Ibid.*, p. 73.

[27] *Ibid.*, p. 72.

[28] *Ibid.*, p. 75.

[29] See *ibid.*, p. 73. 'This division of a product into a useful thing and a value becomes practically important only when exchange has acquired such an extension that useful articles are produced for the purpose of being exchanged, and their character as values has therefore to be taken into account, beforehand, during production.'

[30] *Ibid.*, p. 77.

[31] G. Lukacs, *History and Class Consciousness* (London: Merlin Press, 1971).

[32] *Ibid.*, p. 83.

[33] See similar arguments in the later works of one of Lukacs's early colleagues, K. Mannheim.

[34] Lukacs, *op. cit.*, p. 103.

[35] P. Berger and S. Pullberg, 'Reification and the sociological critique of consciousness', *New Left Review*, no. 35 (January-February 1966).

[36] *Ibid.*, p. 67. The Durkheimian emphasis is quite deliberate on the part of the authors. I take up their analysis again in Part III(B).

[37] Lukacs, *op. cit.*, p. 87.

[38] Marx, *op. cit.*, p. 73 (my emphasis).

[39] *Ibid.*, p. 72 (my emphasis).

[40] *Ibid.*, p. 76.

[41] *Ibid.*, p. 80.

[42] G. Stedman-Jones, 'The marxism of the early Lukacs', *New Left Review*, no. 70 (November-December 1971), pp. 48-9.

[43] Lukacs, *op. cit.*, p. 164.

[44] Marx, *op. cit.*, p. 542.

[45] Althusser, *For Marx*: Harmondsworth, Penguin Books (1969). See Part II(C) for further discussion of Althusser's concept of ideology.

PART II: 5. THE CONCEPT OF MODE OF PRODUCTION

[1] K. Marx, *Capital* (London: Lawrence and Wishart, 1970), vol. 1, p. 239.

[2] *Ibid.*, p. 235. See also p. 270.

[3] *Ibid.*, p. 84.

[4] G. A. Cohen, 'On some criticisms of Historical Materialism', *Supplementary Proceedings of the Aristotelian Society*, vol. 44 (1970), p. 138.

[5] L. Althusser and E. Balibar, *Reading Capital* (London: New Left Books, 1970), p. 97.

[6] My discussion is actually drawn largely from parts of *Reading Capital* that are written by Balibar, especially pp. 212ff. However Althusser clearly agrees with Balibar's discussion in his own much shorter account (pp. 170–81 and footnote on p. 174). See also the very clear discussion, largely based on Balibar, in N. Poulantzas, *Political Power and Social Classes* (London: New Left Books, 1973), pp. 25–30.

[7] Althusser and Balibar, *op. cit.*, p. 215.

[8] *Ibid.*, p. 230, author's emphasis.

[9] *Ibid.*, p. 177.

[10] L. Althusser, *For Marx* (Harmondsworth: Penguin Books, 1969), p. 113.

[11] Marx, *op. cit.*, vol. 1, p. 81n., quoted in Althusser and Balibar, *op. cit.*, p. 217.

[12] Althusser, *op. cit.*, p. 111.

[13] *Ibid.*, p. 101, quoted in A. Callinicos, *Althusser's Marxism* (London: Pluto Press, 1976), p. 52.

[14] N. Poulantzas, 'On Social Classes', *New Left Review*, no. 78 (March–April 1973), p. 33.

[15] See Poulantzas, *Political Power and Social Classes*.

[16] Althusser, *op. cit.*, pp. 115–16.

[17] B. Hindess and P. Q. Hirst, *Pre-Capitalist Modes of Production* (London: Routledge and Kegan Paul, 1975). In their later work their position has changed significantly. See, particularly, A. Cutler, B. Hindess, P. Hirst and A. Hussain, *Marx's 'Capital' and Capitalism Today* (London: Routledge and Kegan Paul, 1977). My purpose in discussing Hindess and Hirst's early work is not to review their contributions *per se*, but rather to use it as an illustration of a particular view of the relationship of ideology and economy.

[18] *Ibid.*, p. 2. But see the criticisms advanced by T. Asad and W. Wolpe in their review article, 'Concepts of modes of production', *Economy and Society*, vol. 5, no. 6 (1976). See also the article by J. Banaji, 'Modes of production in a materialist conception of history', *Capital and Class*, no. 3 (Autumn 1977).

[19] Hindess and Hirst, *op. cit.*, pp. 9–10.

[20] The authors are more or less following Althusser here: 'mode of production = articulated combination of a specific mode of appropriation of the social product and a specific mode of appropriation of nature' (*ibid.*, p. 125).

[21] *Ibid.*, p. 14.

[22] *Ibid.*, p. 124.

[23] *Ibid.*, p. 129.

[24] *Ibid.*, p. 132.

[25] M. Weber, *The Protestant Ethic and the Spirit of Capitalism* (London: Allen and Unwin, 1965).

[26] *Ibid.*, p. 17.

[27] *Ibid.*, p. 91.

[28] *Ibid.*, p. 72.

[29] Hindess and Hirst, *op. cit.*, p. 148.

[30] Althusser and Balibar, *op. cit.*, p. 174 (authors' emphasis).

[31] Marx, *op. cit.*, vol. 1, p. 85.

[32] K. Marx and F. Engels, *The Communist Manifesto* in their *Selected Works* (London: Lawrence and Wishart, 1970), p. 35.

[33] Poulantzas, *Political Power and Social Classes*, p. 62.

[34] Poulantzas, 'On Social Classes', p. 28.

[35] See, for example, R. Crompton and J. Gubbay, *Economy and Class Structure* (London: Macmillan, 1977).

[36] I cannot go into the technicalities of arguments about the development of capitalism and the State. See J. Holloway and S. Picciotto (eds.), *State and Capital* (London: Edward Arnold, 1978).

[37] For discussion of the logic of similar kinds of argument, the reader should refer back to Part I(A).

[38] A Foster-Carter, 'The modes of production debate', *New Left Review*, no. 107 (January-February 1978), p. 55.

PART II: 6. HEGEMONY AND THE HUMAN SUBJECT

[1] See N. Abercrombie, S. Hill and B. Turner, *The Dominant Ideology Thesis* (London: Allen and Unwin, forthcoming, 1980).

[2] See Part I(A).

[3] Gramsci wrote much of his best-known work in a series of notebooks. The difficulties of interpretation are enormous and well known. There is no really adequate account of Gramsci's work as a whole but two articles, largely on his concept of hegemony, are useful. These are: P. Anderson, 'The Antimonies of Antonio Gramsci', *New Left Review*, no. 100 (November 1976/January 1977) and J. Femia, 'Hegemony and Consciousness in the thought of Antonio Gramsci', *Political Studies*, vol. 23, no. 1 (1973).

[4] G. Williams, 'Egemonia in the Thought of Antonio Gramsci', *Journal of the History of Ideas* (October-December 1960). Quoted in Femia, *op. cit.*, p. 31.

[5] A. Gramsci, *Selections from the Prison Notebooks*, edited by Q. Hoare and G. Nowell-Smith (London: Lawrence and Wishart, 1971), p. 161.

[6] *Ibid.*, p. 238.

[7] I am indebted to P. Anderson, *op. cit.*, for much of the discussion here. Actually, Anderson indicates that Gramsci had three accounts of hegemony, of which the one presented here is the most significant.

[8] A. Gramsci, *Quaderni del Carcere* (Turin: vol. 2), p. 1049, quoted in Anderson, *op. cit.*, p. 32.

[9] N. Poulantzas, *Political Power and Social Classes* (London: New Left Books, 1973), pp. 207-8. Author's emphasis.

[10] Gramsci, *Prison Notebooks*, pp. 57-8.

[11] *Ibid.*, p. 366.

[12] A. Callinicos, *Althusser's Marxism* (London: Pluto Press, 1976), p. 49.

[13] P. Hirst, 'Althusser and the theory of ideology', *Economy and Society*, vol. 5, no. 4 (1976), pp. 385-6.

[14] L. Althusser, 'Ideology and Ideological State Apparatuses', in his *Lenin and Philosophy* (London: New Left Books, 1971).

[15] G. McLennan, V. Molina and R. Peters, 'Althusser's Theory of Ideology', in *Working Papers No. 10: On Ideology* (Birmingham: Centre for Contemporary Cultural Studies, 1977).

[16] Althusser, *op. cit.*, p. 126.

[17] *Ibid.*, pp. 127-8.

[18] *Ibid.*, p. 142.

[19] *Ibid.*, p. 148.

[20] *Ibid.*, p. 139.

[21] Hirst, *op. cit.*, p. 394.

[22] I am not convinced that Hirst can resolve these tensions. See Abercrombie, Hill and Turner, *op. cit.*

[23] L. Althusser, *For Marx* (Hardmondsworth: Penguin Books, 1969), p. 232.

[24] *Ibid.*, p. 235.

[25] Althusser, 'Ideology and Ideological State Apparatuses', p. 155.

[26] Althusser, *For Marx*, p. 234. Author's emphasis.

[27] Althusser, 'Ideology and Ideological State Apparatuses', p. 160.

[28] *Ibid.*, p. 163.

[29] See for example, the journal *Ideology and Consciousness*, R. Coward and J. Ellis, *Language and Materialism* (London: Routledge and Kegan Paul, 1977), B. Hindess and P. Hirst, *Mode of Production and Social Formation* (London: Macmillan, 1977) and L. Althusser, *Essays in self-criticism* (London: New Left Books, 1976).

[30] See T. B. Bottomore, 'Some Reflections on the Sociology of Knowledge', *British Journal of Sociology*, vol. 7 (1956).

[31] E. Shils, *The Intellectuals and the Powers and other Essays* (Chicago: University of Chicago Press, 1972), p. 4.

[32] Gramsci, *Prison Notebooks*, p. 9.

[33] *Ibid.*, p. 5.

[34] *Ibid.*, p. 5.

[35] A. Gramsci, *Il Risorgimento* (Turin: 1966), quoted in T. R. Bates, 'Gramsci and the theory of hegemony', *Journal of the History of Ideas*, vol. 36, no. 2 (1975), p. 353.

[36] J. P. Nettl, 'Ideas, Intellectuals, and structures of dissent', in P. Rieff (ed.), *On Intellectuals* (New York: Doubleday, 1970).

PART III: 7. SCHUTZ

[1] M. Speier, 'Phenomenology and social theory: discovering actors and social acts', *Berkely Journal of Sociology*, vol. 12 (1967).

[2] See, for example, the arguments in B. Smart, *Sociology, Phenomenology and Marxian Analysis* (London: Routledge and Kegan Paul, 1976).

[3] An argument put in many ethnomethodological writings. See, for example, H. Sacks, 'Sociological description', *Berkeley Journal of Sociology*, vol. 8 (1963).

[4] Mostly in A. Schutz, *The Phenomenology of the Social World* (London: Heinemann Educational Books, 1972) and A. Schutz, *Collected Papers*, vols. 1 and 2 (The Hague: Nijhoff, 1971) (hereafter CP).

[5] Mostly in CP vols 1 and 2 and A. Schutz, *The Structures of the Life-World* (London: Heinemann Educational Books, 1974) (hereafter SLW).

[6] See, for example, the essays, 'Common-sense and scientific interpretation of human action' and 'Concept and theory formation in the social sciences' in CP vol. 1. Most of the critical literature has concentrated on this question of scientificity.

[7] 'Common-sense and scientific interpretation of human nature', CP vol. 1, p. 35.

[8] *Ibid.*, p. 35.

[9] SLW, p. 3.

[10] *Ibid.*, p. 4.

[11] CP vol. 1, p. 230.

[12] CP vol. 2, pp. 72–3.

[13] For further elucidation of these terms, see SLW Chapter 2, section B.

[14] H. R. Wagner (ed.), *Alfred Schütz on Phenomenology and Social Relations* (Chicago: University of Chicago Press, 1970), p. 225.

[15] *Ibid.*, p. 225 (emphasis added).

[16] *Ibid.*, p. 116.

[17] *Ibid.*, p. 112.

[18] CP vol. 1, p. 5.

[19] Wagner, *op. cit.*, pp. 111–12.

[20] J. Heeren, 'Alfred Schütz and the sociology of common-sense knowledge', in J. Douglas (ed.), *Understanding Everyday Life* (London: Routledge and Kegan Paul, 1971).

[21] It is unfortunate in this respect that this book was compiled by Luckmann from Schutz's notes after his death, for Luckmann holds a very particular view of the relationship of the individual and social structure.

[22] CP vol. 1, p. 218.

[23] SLW, p. 261.

[24] *Ibid.*, p. 246. Note Schutz's interesting use of the notion of institution.

[25] P. Popkin, 'Where are the living? A critical review of the *Collected Papers* of Alfred Schutz', *Berkeley Journal of Sociology*, vol. 12 (1967).

[26] R. Gorman, *The Dual Vision* (London: Routledge and Kegan Paul, 1977). In my view, Gorman understates Schutz's emphasis on the role of social determinations.

[27] See Smart, *op. cit.*, pp. 101–4.

PART III: 8. BERGER AND LUCKMANN

[1] See, for example, P. Berger, *The Social Reality of Religion* (London: Faber and Faber, 1969), P. Berger, 'Identity as a problem in the sociology of knowledge', in J. E. Curtis and J. Petras (eds.), *The Sociology of Knowledge* (London: Duckworth, 1970), P. Berger, B. Berger and H. Kellner, *The Homeless Mind* (Harmondsworth: Penguin Books, 1974), P. Berger and T. Luckmann, 'Sociology of religion and sociology of knowledge', *Sociology and Social Research*, vol. 47, no. 4 (1963), P. Berger and S. Pullberg, 'Reification and the sociological critique of consciousness', *New Left Review*, no. 35 (January-February 1966), T. Luckmann, *The Invisible Religion* (New York: Collier-Macmillan, 1970).

[2] P. Berger and T. Luckmann, *The Social Construction of Reality* (London: Allen Lane, 1967), p. 26.

[3] *Ibid.*, p. 49.

[4] *Ibid.*, p. 30.

[5] Berger, *Social Reality of Religion*, p. 4.

[6] Berger and Luckmann, *op. cit.*, p. 65.

[7] *Ibid.*, p. 65.

[8] *Ibid.*, p. 60.

[9] Berger, *Social Reality of Religion*, p. 22.

[10] Berger and Luckmann, *op. cit.*, p. 72.

[11] *Ibid.*, p. 74.

[12] *Ibid.*, p. 75.

[13] *Ibid.*, p. 78

[14] *Ibid.*, p. 116.

[15] *Ibid.*, p. 121.

[16] See Berger and Luckmann, 'Sociology of religion and sociology of knowledge'.

[17] Luckmann, *The Invisible Religion*.

[18] See Berger, *Social Reality of Religion*, Chapter 4.

[19] *Ibid.*, p. 30.

[20] I. Light, 'The social construction of uncertainty', *Berkeley Journal of Sociology*, vol. 14 (1969).

[21] Berger and Luckmann, *op. cit.*, p. 140.

[22] *Ibid.*, p. 153.

[23] In the view of Berger and Luckmann, asymmetry between subjective and objective realities depends on the social structure, and varies particularly as between simple and complex societies. See Berger and Luckmann, *op. cit.*, pp. 183–93.

[24] Berger, *op. cit.*, p. 84.

[25] Berger and Luckmann, *op. cit.*, p. 167.

[26] *Ibid.*, p. 167.

[27] H. Garfinkel, *Studies in Ethnomethodology* (Englewood Cliffs: Prentice-Hall, 1967).

[28] H. Garfinkel, 'A conception of, and experiments with, "trust" as a condition of stable concerted actions', in O. J. Harvey (ed.), *Motivation and Social Interaction* (New York: the Ronald Press, 1963).

[29] For example, Berger, *op. cit.*, p. 24: 'Every socially defined reality remains threatened by lurking "irrealities". Every socially constructed nomos must face the constant possibility of its collapse into anomy. Seen in the perspective of society, every nomos is an area of meaning carved out of a vast mass of meaninglessness, a small clearing of lucidity in a formless, dark, always ominous, jungle. Seen in the perspective of the individual, every nomos represents the bright "dayside" of life, fervently held onto against the sinister shadows of the "night".'

[30] Berger *et al.*, *The Homeless Mind*, p. 62.

[31] Berger, *op. cit.*, p. 18.

[32] Berger and Luckmann, *op. cit.*, p. 80.

[33] R. Robertson, *The Sociological Interpretation of Religion* (Oxford: Basil Blackwell, 1970), p. 201.

PART III: CONCLUSION

[1] P. Berger and T. Luckmann, *The Social Construction of Reality* (London: Allen Lane, 1967), p. 27.

[2] As Althusser describes his critique of theories of ideology:
'Disappeared: The term ideas
Survive: The terms subject, consciousness, belief, actions.
Appear: The terms practices, rituals, ideological apparatus'
L. Althusser, *Lenin and Philosophy* (London: New Left Review Edition, 1977), p. 159.

[3] Epistemology = Theory of the grounds of knowledge.
Ontology   = Theory of the essence of things.

[4] N. Poulantzas, *Political Power and Social Classes* (London: New Left Books, 1973), p. 209.

[5] R. Miliband, *The State in Capitalist Society* (London Weidenfeld and Nicolson, 1969), pp. 180, 182. Author's emphasis.

[6] See for example, the critique of Hindess and Hirst's earlier work by T. Asad and H. Wolpe, 'Concepts of modes of production', *Economy and Society*, vol. 5 no. 6 (1976).
See also B. S. Turner, 'The structuralist critique of Weber's Sociology', *British Journal of Sociology*, vol. 28, no. 1 (1977).

[7] See B. Barnes, *Scientific Knowledge and Sociological Theory* (London: Routledge and Kegan Paul, 1974).

[8] W. Stark, *The Sociology of Knowledge* (London: Routledge and Kegan Paul, 1958), p. 274.

Ibid., p. 278.

[10] P. Q. Hirst, 'Althusser and the theory of ideology', *Economy and Society*, vol. 5, no. 4 (1976), p. 386.

[11] The Editorial Collective, 'Psychology, ideology, and the human subject', *Ideology and Consciousness*, no. 1 (May 1977), p. 21.

[12] See L. Althusser, 'Ideology and Ideological State Apparatuses', in his *Lenin and Philosophy*, *op. cit*. But also see *Ideology and Consciousness*, *op. cit.*, pp. 22–4, and S. Hall, 'Some problems with the ideology/subject couplet', *Ideology and Consciousness*, no. 3 (Spring 1978).

[13] K. Mannheim, 'On Conservative Thought', in his *Essays on Sociology and Social Psychology* (London Routledge and Kegan Paul, 1953.

[14] M. Seeman, 'Intellectual perspective and adjustment to minority status', in J. Curtis and J. W. Petras (eds.), *The Sociology of Knowledge* (London: Duckworth, 1970).

[15] V. K. Dibble, 'Occupations and Ideologies', in Curtis and Petras, *op. cit.*

[16] R. K. Merton, 'Science and Economy of 17th Century England', in

his *Social Theory and Social Structure* (New York: The Free Press, 1975).

[17] See B. Barnes, *Interests and the Growth of Knowledge* (London: Routledge and Kegan Paul, 1977).

[18] See Hirst, *op. cit.*

[19] For a more extensive discussion of these points see N. Abercrombie, S. Hill and B. S. Turner, *The Dominant Ideology Thesis* (London: Allen and Unwin, forthcoming), Chapter 6.

[20] For discussion of the functionalism of this argument, see Part I(A).

[21] The whole subject of how to theorize class in relation to the mode of production is a controversial area. See Poulantzas, *op. cit.*, E. O. Wright, *Class, Crisis and The State* London: New Left Books, 1978) and A. Cutler *et al.*; *Marx's Capital and Capitalism Today* (London: Routledge and Kegan Paul, 1977).

[22] See Part II(A).

[23] H. Neisser, *On the Sociology of Knowledge* (New York: Heineman, 1965), p. 24.

[24] Althusser holds an extreme form of this argument. He argues that beliefs held cannot be illusions by comparison with the real because there is no way that we can have contact with the real independently of the theories that we hold about it. Hence, since the real cannot be perceived at all, our perceptions of it must take the form of 'imaginary' representations, i.e. ideology. There clearly is a real epistemological difference between this theory and that which forms the basis for the conventional sociology of knowledge. I take the view that Althusser's epistemology is relativist, but see A. Callinicos, *Althusser's Marxism* (London: Pluto Press, 1976).

Index